GOD'S WATER CARRIER

Susannah Ralph

Kingdom Publishers

Copyright© Susannah Ralph 2023

All rights reserved. No part of this book may be reproduced in any form by photocopying or any electronic or mechanical means, including information storage or retrieval systems, without permission in writing from both the copyright owner and the publisher of the book. The right of Susannah Ralph to be identified as the author of this work has been asserted by her in accordance with the Copyright, Designs and Patents Act 1988 and any subsequent amendments thereto.

A catalogue record for this book is available from the

British Library.

All Scripture Quotations have been taken from the New Kings James version of the Bible and the complete Jewish Bible.

ISBN: 978-1-911697-95-4

1st Edition 2023 by Kingdom Publishers, London, UK.

You can purchase copies of this book from any leading bookstore or email **contact@kingdompublishers.co.uk**

Dedication

I would like to dedicate this book to my husband who is always there when I need him, and to all my friends who have encouraged me in this endeavour especially close friends that know me well and know my heart for God.

I also want to dedicate this book to my friend Donne, who went to be with the Lord a few years ago.

God I want to be Your Water Carrier...

This book is written to glorify God and to show ordinary people what He can do with somebody that has a willing and open heart.

Thank you, Lord Jesus and Holy Spirit, for the privilege of being used in the ways that only You could have chosen.

Thank you for prompting me to draw from my journals and create this book. May it encourage others to be obedient and faithful and to do that which You have called them to do.

As you read this book, believe me when I say that you are not reading it by accident. God always has a plan, and He has a plan for your life too.

Scriptures used are taken from COMPLETE JEWISH BIBLE (CJB) Copyright © 1998 by David H. Stern. All rights reserved.

THE NEW KING JAMES VERSION® (NKJV). Copyright© 1982 by Thomas Nelson, Inc. USA

THE MESSAGE Copyright©1993, 1994, 1995, 1996, 2000 by NavPress Publishing Group, USA

"My Devotional", "Daily reading" etc. refer to YouVersion Bible® App – Daily Devotional by Life Church Publications, Oklahoma, USA

I have attempted as much as possible to cite all my sources and references but many are from what I have learned or heard in the past so I apologise if any citation is either incomplete or has been omitted all together.

© 2023 Susannah E. Ralph, Wales, UK

Artwork by Peter John Carter

Contents

Introduction	9
CHAPTER ONE | Encountering God	13
CHAPTER TWO | The Start of My Journey	15
CHAPTER THREE | Meeting the Holy Spirit	17
CHAPTER FOUR | Healing Touches	19
CHAPTER FIVE | New Seasons	35
CHAPTER SIX | Going to the UK for Christmas	43
CHAPTER SEVEN | The Fast	48
CHAPTER EIGHT | New Direction	51
CHAPTER NINE | Birth Days	54
CHAPTER TEN | What's Next Lord	60
CHAPTER ELEVEN | A Brand New Season and New Year	64
CHAPTER TWELVE | Spending Time with Jesus	67
CHAPTER THIRTEEN | My Testimony	70
CHAPTER FOURTEEN | First Fruits Fasting	73
CHAPTER FIFTEEN | Being Ready to Hear and to Do	77
CHAPTER SIXTEEN | The Crossing Over	82
CHAPTER SEVENTEEN | Celebrations for the Nations	86
CHAPTER EIGHTEEN | A Jubilee Year	93
CHAPTER NINETEEN | Behold, I will Do a New Thing	99
CHAPTER TWENTY | The Gatekeeper	106
CHAPTER TWENTY-ONE | Butterflies and Transformation	110
CHAPTER TWENTY-TWO | A New Season	113

CHAPTER TWENTY-THREE | Yom Kippur   122
CHAPTER TWENTY-FOUR | Hiddenness and Manifestation   125
CHAPTER TWENTY-FIVE | A Year of Progress and Acceleration   129
CHAPTER TWENTY-SIX | Praying for Open Doors   139
CHAPTER TWENTY-SEVEN | When God Gives a New Name   142
CHAPTER TWENTY-EIGHT | The Battle is The Lord's   148
CHAPTER TWENTY-NINE | Times and Seasons   153
CHAPTER THIRTY | All Change   162
CHAPTER THIRTY-ONE | A Year of Knocking on Doors   178
CHAPTER THIRTY-TWO | In the Waiting Room   189

Introduction

My journey with God started around March – April 2002. It was Ian's 50th birthday and I was back in the UK having flown back to visit my daughter, Jayne, for a couple of weeks.

I phoned Ian to wish him a happy birthday; it was the first time that we were not together for a celebration.

Imagine my surprise when a woman answered his mobile phone and told me that he had been in a terrible car accident. My younger daughter, Paula, was with me and when she heard that her dad had been in an accident, she became very upset and so both girls went into the kitchen while I called back a second time to make sure I had the right number.

The doctor in question just said, "Your husband has been in an accident, please phone back in ten minutes; I am trying to stabilise him," and then put the phone down.

The girls were now in the kitchen and I remember looking up at the ceiling in the lounge and saying, "God, I have lost one daughter and I cannot lose my husband!"

That was the first time I had called out to a God that I did not know anything about, or so I thought.

We had lost our older daughter in South Africa, and I could not handle the fact that Ian was not in a good way, neither could Paula, after all he is her dad.

After a little while, she calmed down and started phoning the airline to get me an emergency flight back to South Africa and she would follow later.

I arrived back three days later and when I arrived at the hospital, I was told that Ian had been unconscious since the crash and had just woken up.

When I arrived, I found two acquaints (who later became friends), there with him and they had been looking after his needs until I arrived back.

We had bought our businesses from them individually; Ian's being a paint business and mine an Interiors business.

Later they invited us to go to church with them as none of us had any knowledge of God whatsoever, but in saying that I had called out to God in my distress back in the UK.

So out of gratitude for helping Ian we decide to go with them to church.

The minute I stepped into the church, I was overwhelmed, and tears began to stream down my face although I did not understand why.

For the next three weeks it happened the same way, I could not get through a song without weeping. Around the third week, as the Pastor gave an altar call to receive Jesus Christ as Lord and Saviour, I submitted and said, "Yes Lord, I need You to be my saviour."

As I did, I saw Jesus standing in front of me with His arms open wide. He stepped forward and hugged me. There was such a strong feeling of love that I have never forgotten it.

Jesus hugged me and welcomed me into the Kingdom of God.

What I did not know until later was that Ian had given his life to Christ the same day. We both went on to be baptised in water and in the Spirit and we both received the gift of tongues.

I can only speak for myself when I say that I felt God had taken me, shaken me, turned me inside out and pointed me in the opposite direction.

Before I met the Lord, I was not in a good place, I drank a lot (probably too much) and I also swore a lot, my language was very blue to say the least, of which I am not proud I would like to add.

However, when I had that meeting with Jesus, suddenly I stopped swearing to the point that even my manager said that he did not recognise me as the same person.

I remember him saying to me, "Sue, what has happened to you? you are a completely different person!"

I shared with him that I have given my life to Christ and become a Christian. I realised there was still a lot of work to be done in me, but I was told that, that would come as I committed myself to walk with the Lord.

Jesus had become the Lord of my life and now the journey of teaching and training me in His ways could start.

I must be honest here I did not realise how much training I would need or how hard it would be at times, but I was determined that I would follow Him and not go back to where I was before. I am so grateful that He took me out of darkness and gave me His glorious Light.

Amazing Grace how sweet the sound that saved a wretch like me,

I once was lost and now I am found was blind but now I see.

Thank you, Abba, Lord Jesus and Holy Spirit.

CHAPTER ONE | Encountering God

When I first met the Lord, I wanted to know His story. We all have stories of how things happened in our lives, and I believe the bible is God's story.

He formed a people for Himself to bless and be a blessing to others.

When I read the bible for the first time, I was amazed at His story and so I read it through a second time. I read all the way through from Genesis to Revelation.

As I read, it was as if I was there, it was so real and things started jumping out at me, things I did not know about, God was giving me revelations.

I remember my first encounter with God a few weeks later.

We had been asked to host a baptism at our home as the people who normally did it were away on leave. I started preparing the house making sure that everything was neat and tidy, as I started mopping the floors I suddenly started to shake and weep.

As nothing like this had ever happened to me at home before, I asked a question, "Lord is that You?" I wanted to make sure that it was Him.

Suddenly I heard a voice saying, "You are a Christian and you are surrounded by Egyptians."

A few years earlier, we had taken a holiday in Egypt and of course had bought numerous touristy Items, including papyruses, which we hung on the walls of our lounge and dining room. I also had a bust of Tutankhamun as a table centre and other keepsakes of the sphinx and pyramids in my wall cabinets.

As all these things seemed to fill my mind, with tears streaming down my face, the voice spoke a second time. "You are a Christian, but you are surrounded by Egyptians!"

Believing it was the Lord speaking to me, I asked again, "Lord is that You? What do You want me to do?"

I did not hear anything audibly, but I knew deep down that I had to take everything off the walls. Through the tears, I took down all the papyruses from the walls, and all the other items and I put them into the home office until Ian came home from work.

Ian's first reaction was not what I thought it would be and he put everything back on the walls. My first instinct was to ask the Lord for forgiveness and ask Him to speak to Ian's heart.

About a week later, Ian asked if I really wanted to get rid of everything and with what I would replace the items in question.

I said that I would decide and if that is what God wants us to do then we should do it. We then together took everything out of the house and destroyed it or burned it. We had help from our church intercessors and cell group leaders; they also taught us how to carry out spiritual house cleaning.

Later the Lord led us through the house and showed us all the things that needed to be cleared out that were displeasing to Him.

God not only wanted to dwell in our hearts but to dwell in our home as well. He wanted His manifest presence to be recognised when people visited us. Everyone commented on how peaceful our home was when they visited and said they could sense God's presence when they entered the front door. What a privilege and honour.

Thank you, Lord God, Lord Jesus, and Holy Spirit.

CHAPTER TWO | **The Start of My Journey**

Quite a while later, I was baptised in the Holy Spirit, and what felt like an explosion from deep within me came out of my mouth in a language I had not spoken before, it came with such an intense feeling of joy and happiness, with tears pouring down my face.

My friend who had been praying for me looked on amazed at what God was doing!

It was an amazing moment that will live with me always, the only way I could describe it, is that it was like a volcano erupting and only something that God could do.

One morning as I was preparing to sit with the Lord, I suddenly had an open vision. As I had made some tea, I suddenly saw myself stood by the side of Jesus. I saw a long line of people standing in my dining room and kitchen; it was strange as I could see right through them like holograms.

I asked the Lord what I was looking at to which He replied, "These people are all the people that you will be praying for!"

The line of people did not get shorter as people seemed to keep joining the end of the queue. It was wonderful to watch but again I wondered what it meant for me and my journey with God. As I was watching and looking, I tried to see more, but the vision started to fade, and I was left to contemplate.

I wanted to learn everything that God wanted to teach me, and in the years that followed, He taught me so much. He did not teach me just through His word, but He also taught me through obedience to Him as He sent me out with different assignments.

I learned to sit with Him in the mornings daily and listen for His voice. I learned that when He says something, He means it.

I learned that I could trust Him and that He does what He says He will do. Over the next eight years, God was training me to see His heart and know Him.

CHAPTER THREE | Meeting the Holy Spirit

God started to introduce me to the work of the Holy Spirit and as I sat with Him, He would give me, an assignment (what I like to call a DVD). He would show me precisely what to do and how to do it. I cannot say it was always easy to approach people that I had never met, but it was always worth it just to see Him at work in their lives.

As I was learning then He started giving me visions, again I can only say that it was in DVD form, I would see the whole thing and then go out to do what He had shown me.

He would speak to me in dreams and give me revelations of seeking the Kingdom of God first and foremost.

One morning, as I sat with the Lord, I was suddenly transported onto a beach (in the spirit). I saw Jesus cooking breakfast just as He had cooked fish for the disciples. He said, "Come and have breakfast with Me!"

He gave me revelation of seeking His Kingdom first and His righteousness and that everything will be added unto you.

This was an amazing time with the Lord and as we sat on the beach, I realised it was the beach at Tiberias in Israel, it actually became more real as my husband and I went to Israel eight years later and I was able to put my feet in the water there. He said, "Come and eat my food and drink the wine I have mixed,"

Song of Solomon 5:19 (to His friends) Eat, O friends! Drink, yes, drink deeply, O beloved ones!

When I opened my eyes, I was still sitting in the lounge with my cat on my lap and a cup of coffee in my hand.

This was a wonderful start of my walk with the Lord and there was more to come.

CHAPTER FOUR | Healing Touches

Starting a new year with the Lord is always exciting in the way He speaks to us and shows us what He is going to do. It is not normally the way we think, as His ways are not ours. At the beginning of this year, God decided to give me a new name. I was led by the Holy Spirit to read Isaiah 62:3-5, which reads as follows.

You will be a glorious crown in the hand of Adonai, a royal diadem held by your God, you will no longer be spoken of as 'abandoned' or your land be spoken of as 'desolate,' rather you will be called Hephzibah (My delight is in her) and your land 'Beulah.' for Adonai delights in you.

Although I did not hear an audible voice, I heard deep in my heart God say to me, "Make your flesh ready as the blessings that I am going to pour out on you will be so much that you will not cope if you do not prepare yourself..... PREPARE YOURSELF."

As I sat and pondered on what that entailed and what it meant, I started to prepare my heart by sitting at Jesus feet and listening for His voice and for any instruction.

On Monday evenings, it was our regular practice to go through all the worship songs ready for the following Sunday service.

I had been in the worship group for a while and had become very good friends with Donne, one of the other backup singers. Donne had fallen at the back of the platform a few weeks earlier and had broken her wrist in three places. She was in a lot of pain and had been crying out to God for healing as she had been for x-rays in the morning, and they had shown no healing in her wrist after three whole weeks.

As we sat praying before worship started, I heard a very quiet voice in my right ear saying to me, "Tell Donne, by My stripes she is healed."

It was so quiet that I asked, "Is that You Lord?" and a second time I heard the same voice say the same thing.

"Tell Donne by My stripes she is healed."

Prayer time was coming to an end and as we walked into our positions at the microphones, I said to her what God had told me. Imagine as I started to speak, we both felt the presence of God so strong that I can only describe it as lightning coming down from heaven.

Our feet were both pinned to the floor, we could not move, my hand was so hot that Donne said to me, "Sue your hand is getting so hot!"

I sheepishly replied, "Donne, God is healing your wrist!"

I do not know which of us was more surprised as we had not prayed for healing except to say that I believe God gave me a word of knowledge and He had carried it out. We just looked at each other not knowing what to say but after what seemed like an age, which was probably only between 10-20 seconds, her wrist was healed and she had no more pain.

The following day she was booked to have new plaster put onto her arm and even though she had the experience of healing, she decided to go to the hospital as she had not told anyone what had happened. A week later, she had to take her daughter to the hospital for another appointment, but her plaster was so uncomfortable that the doctor decided to cut it off and send her for x-rays to find out more.

When the x-rays came back, they showed that there was nothing wrong with her wrist and that it had totally healed. The doctor asked her, "Donne what is wrong with your wrist?"

After telling the doctor the whole story she realised God had done what He said, and had healed her wrist. She also realised that she now had proof as she had two sets of x-rays, the first one showing her wrist broken in three places, and a week later, a second set showing her wrist totally healed.

We gave God all the glory and thanks and it built our faith tremendously. We also prayed for her daughter who was also in pain due to a procedure that she was having done. Again, God came through and touched her amazingly.

God was teaching me that the power of His word is conceived in our hearts, and then formed by the tongue and when we are obedient to speak it as He instructs, it becomes a force releasing the ability of God in us.

God is compassionate. He gave both mother and daughter the strength they needed at the right time.

We all have stories in our lives and as we walk with God, He will open the story of our life to us. I see the bible as God's story from the beginning to the end; this book is part of my life story with Him.

My friend and I would regularly get together for a worship session at her home and, as usual, we decided to hold a morning session. When I arrived, I wondered why the guitar stand etc. had not been set up, as she was always organised.

We made coffee and then retired into the lounge, suddenly Leslie came into the room and said, "Sue I have a word from God for you, and I am praying that I don't get it wrong!"

God had laid this on her heart, and she had written it down so that she would remember everything that He had said. I also heard in my spirit as we prayed and gave the time to Him: Remember this day - it was the 20.1.2007.

This is what she believed God had told her to say to me, and when she started to speak, it was as if He was right there with us; His presence was so tangible.

The word was:

He was giving me a healing ministry, and that money would never be a problem for me.

For me to remember that He always gets the glory.

I need to stay childlike and be obedient.

I must be careful to whom I testify and not to cast my pearls before swine.

My husband, Ian, will be raised up to support what the Lord has called us to do.

God had already started using me to heal people so I took this as a confirmation of my calling, or at least part of it.

The Lord had spoken to me about sharing daily communion with Him, which I took to mean that we break bread together every day, something that is still ongoing in my life.

We need to watch our egos lest we become too full of ourselves. We need to humble ourselves under His Mighty hand as we have nothing of ourselves to offer anyone.

Faith operates in two places, heart and mouth.

I remember when God said to me one day, if you cannot say something good about somebody, then do not say anything at all. He said this as I used to be a very negative person. I could only see the negative instead of looking for the positive.

God gave me a picture of a laser beam coming out of my mouth; it opened up and was full of words. God asked, "How did I create the world?

Looking up at the ceiling, (I do not know why) I answered Him, "Lord, you spoke it into being! You said, 'Let there be light', and there was light." He then directed me to the scriptures, Genesis 1:3 God said, 'let there be light', and there was light.

He then took me to scriptures about the tongue.

Proverbs 13:2. We eat the fruit of our lips

James 3:9-10 ...with it we curse men who have been made in the similitude of God. Out of the same mouth proceed blessing and cursing. My brethren, these things ought not to be so.

I was so convicted by the Holy Spirit that I repented there and then and asked God to cleanse my mouth, which He did. He helped me change the way I think and to see things from a different perspective.

I learned to speak God's blessing over people as He was teaching me and said that we are blessed to be a blessing. From that day on, I watched my words very carefully. This does not mean to say that I am perfect, but when I stumble, I am quick to repent and ask God to forgive and cleanse me.

Let me share with you another healing assignment that the Holy Spirit had prompted in me. The Holy Spirit often speaks to me when I have my hands in water, although sometimes it is when I am in the shower. This particular day, as I was showering, God started to give me a DVD of a woman in the local hospital. I saw this woman lying down in bed looking really ill. God gave me the scripture in Matthew 9:22 about the woman with the issue of blood. I asked the Lord when I should go to the hospital, and He replied, "Now!"

I had been to Rob Ferreira hospital on more than one occasion, so the staff there knew me well. As I was getting dressed, the Lord instructed me to a wear a specific-coloured blouse.

I dressed and left for the hospital. I had seen myself walking up the steps to the 10th ward and then turning left into a single room. As I approached the ward, I was asked by a nurse if I needed help. I said I did not as I knew where to go. I entered the ward, which I thought was the correct one and you can imagine my surprise to see this woman, sitting up with a beautiful smile.

I was now confused; she did not look like the person God had shown me. That person was lying down, unwell. I walked up and down the ward to make sure I was in the right place. Then, still a bit confused, I went out onto the fire escape to ask God if I had heard correctly. I waited a little while and did not seem to get an answer so I thought I would just go back and speak to her. I lingered outside the ward for what seemed like ages, and she asked if I was looking for somebody.

"I think I am looking for you."

"I think you are too", she replied.

I said good morning, and introduced myself. I asked her if she had a problem with her blood and she proceeded to tell me the whole story of why she was in hospital. Sometimes part of our story is intertwined with other people's story, and this was one of those times.

She said that her son had brought her into hospital the day before because she had been in a diabetic coma. While she was in the coma, she had met Jesus and He had healed her.

I was amazed by her testimony but then I understood why God had given me this scripture for her, also the reason why her smile was so beautiful. The presence of God was awesome to say the least. I felt as if I had known her for years even though I had just met her.

I told her I believed God had asked me to come and give her this scripture, Matthew 9:22. Be of good cheer daughter; your faith has made you whole. We carried on chatting for a while and we hugged as I said my goodbyes. She thanked me but I always ask the people to thank God as I am only a servant doing what He has asked me to do. There was so much love in the room; it was beautiful to see and to be part of her story.

As I was leaving, having done what I had been asked to do, I stopped and asked her about the blouse I had on; a lovely pale lilac colour. She answered and said it was her favourite colour.

I left the hospital feeling ecstatic about what I had just witnessed. I was in total awe of how God had led me by His Spirit; it was amazing.

In all of this, we need to remember that God is God and that we need to revere Him and not take Him for granted. The word of God says the Fear of the Lord is the beginning of wisdom. (Proverbs 9:10)

God had sent me out quite a few times with different assignments, but little did I know that He was about to teach me a different lesson, one which I will never forget.

I worked at an interior decorating company having closed my own business. Everyone there was a Christian and it had a lovely vibe to work in. I had also started a programme at church, teaching about physical healing. Even though God had sent me out with different tasks to complete for Him, I knew that I had so much more to learn. Sometimes when we do things for God, we can get overconfident and run ahead of Him. When we read how Jesus performed miracles, we find that He did not do things the same every time. I had found it easy in the past few months as God had given me specific instruction, so not knowing any different, I thought it would always be easy. WRONG!

God was going to give me a lesson on doing what He asks but leaving the results to Him, also giving me more understanding of how He works.

I arrived at work one morning and I answered a phone call from one of the team. She wanted to know if I would go to the hospital to pray for her father. Her father had been diagnosed with lung cancer and she had taken him for radium treatment.

I asked permission from my boss and headed out to the hospital. I had already prayed and asked the Lord if He wanted me to go, and how He wanted me to pray, so I thought, Wow Lord, you are going to heal him so he can be with his family for a few more years. I went to the hospital with great expectation that God was going to heal him.

When I arrived at the hospital, they were in the car park just about to get into the car. I had all the paperwork with me from the healing programme as I asked the Lord, "Where do you want me to start." As I spoke to Amanda's dad, I had a very strong sense to ask if there was anyone he needed to forgive. I very gently said to him, "Sir, I just have a question for you as I feel it is important, is there anyone that you need to forgive?"

As I said this, he started to weep and said there was. I spoke to him gently and asked him to do business with God in his heart and to raise his hand when he was finished. He took his time and after a few minutes, raised his hand so that I could pray for him.

When I had finished, he stood at the side of the car and took a step of faith for his healing, thanking God and giving Him praise. I did everything that I was being taught at church about physical healing, giving to God before I started, so I fully expected it to be achieved and that he would recover. It was just three months later that Amanda's father had passed away and I was so mad at God. I asked Him, "Why did you give me a healing anointing if the people die anyway?" It was the first time God had sent me to pray like this. I was sad as I had really believed he would be healed.

God answered me that day, "My will is My will!"

For a while afterwards I was afraid to pray for people, although I had learned that we pray and leave the results to God. When we pray for people, we need to defer to Him and not have any preconceived ideas.

Isaiah 55:8-9 'For my thoughts are not your thoughts, and your ways are not my ways,' says Adonai. 'As high as the sky is above the earth are my ways higher than your ways, and my thoughts than your thoughts.'

I did repent and ask God to forgive me for not understanding, but I was still learning and learning quickly.

Much later, in 2010, I had a revelation of what God had actually done. It was not about the physical healing but about the unforgiveness that this man had in his heart. All I know is that God is a good God and His heart for us is always good because He does not want anyone to perish; again, it is a choice we make.

As time went by and I grew to know the Lord more, I often went out to pray for and with others. I joined the intercessors group at church and every Friday night we would pray through until 6am.

One such night we were praying and worshipping, enjoying His presence when suddenly I was standing before the Lord and all I could see (with my eyes closed) was a bright light. I was drawn to the light and as I moved closer, I realised it was Jesus. It was so quiet with such power around me that I could not speak. I stood there for what seemed to be so long that eventually I said to the Lord in a whisper, "Lord, I need to go back and pray". It was so surreal, like nothing I had experienced before.

I felt something drop onto my head. I thought it was water as it had been raining outside, but when I opened my eyes, I was in the middle of the hall and everyone was watching me. I heard the Holy Spirit say to me, "I anoint your head with oil!"

Everyone could see that I had been with Jesus. I told them what had happened and then felt the top of my head only to find that it was not water, but oil. One of the leaders then said that Jesus had anointed my head. She also said this from the Lord "You, are My child, the lame will walk, the blind will see, the sick will be healed, and the dead will rise. You will be raised up; you will fly like an eagle."

Psalm 92:11 was the verse God spoke that day. I have anointed you with fresh oil.

God will use us at every opportunity if we are available to hear His voice; even when we are on holiday.

This particular year we decided to change our usual seaside holiday for a resort in the Drakensberg. We had bought a timeshare a few years back and we were eager to use it for a week. Timeshare is a scheme where you buy a week's holiday in different venues each year if there is availability. I contacted the bookings office only to find that there was nothing available for the weekend that we wanted. You can imagine: we were disappointed as we had paid a substantial amount expressly so we could have a holiday every year. We had not been able to use it as often as we would have liked. This would have been a birthday treat as well as a holiday, now we would have to wait to get away later in the year. There was nothing to do but book elsewhere and, of course, pay extra.

Thinking about this and telling God all about it (complaining), I cried, "Lord, we can't afford to pay for something else as we have used our money to buy these timeshares." Still wondering how we would be able to go on a holiday, I received a phone call from a person at the Timeshare head office. He said that although they could not give us the resort we had originally requested they did have availability in another part of the Drakensberg. He also said that, because it was not in our preferred area, they would give it to us at a discount. It was the only available chalet in the Drakensberg for when we wanted. I quickly decided, said yes, and waited to tell Ian as soon as possible. Ian was over the moon; at least we were going to have a break.

We had been to the Drakensberg on one other occasion during which I fell off a horse and hurt my leg. A few years before, we had taken our two small granddaughters along and they asked if they could ride the park horses. I am not a horse person, but I eventually agreed and accompanied them for a ride around the camp. At some point, the horse I was riding became agitated with the one Ian was riding and decided it did not want me on his back. He reared up and tried to throw me off. I was shocked to say the least and, as he threw me off, my leg became entangled in the stirrup. The ranger leading the horses was desperately trying to calm the horses and to help me. My main concern was being trampled. I had undergone a back operation a few years prior and have screws in the base of my spine. Once everything was calm again, I found myself in a heap on the floor with my hands and arms over my head, trying not to be trampled.

The ranger leading us was very concerned and immediately took the horses back to their stables. Unfortunately, there was no site doctor and the nearest one was at least 10kms away. We decided that no one was hurt seriously; all we wanted to do was go back to the chalet and have a cup of tea. Although my back was not hurt, my inside right leg had been stretched, it was swollen and very painful. I did not have any painkillers with me, so I had a warm shower to ease the pain Ian had trained in first aid, and he first placed ice packs onto my inner thigh followed by heat pack to get the swelling down. I remember lying in bed trying to sleep but could not as the pain in my leg was like having toothache.

I cried out to God to relieve the pain, saying, "God, you are my healer. You are Jehovah Rapha." Suddenly God showed up and started to take away the pain. The only way I can describe it is it felt as if He was pulling the pain out of my leg, down through my big toe. As it reached my knee, I was laughing and shouting, "Lord, keep going. It is almost out." I rose out of bed and told Ian what had happened and we thanked the Lord for His grace and healing. The next morning, I woke up and there was no pain or swelling in my leg. This was the first time I had experienced physical healing for myself, and God showed Himself to me in a real way, in a different way, as God my healer.

The date of our break was growing closer and I had this excitement in my heart. It was the middle of the year, time for a break as the beginning of the year always seemed to drag. Isn't it funny that when we are looking forward to something, time seems to go so slow?

Eventually it was time for us to go to the Drakensberg and rest! I remember it was a few hours' drive away and we were both tired, especially from the heat of the day.

We lived in the Highveld, in a place called Secunda. Ian was a miner at that time and I worked as a warehouse manager for a retail company. It felt good to get away into the mountains and breathe fresh air. As we approached the entrance gates of the venue we looked at the view behind us, it was beautiful. We went into the office to book in and just embraced the view; it was God's glorious mountains and so green compared to our own brown dry area.

Once we had been given the key to our chalet, we drove around the complex to where we would be staying, I noticed a man in a wheelchair, sitting just inside the door of his chalet. I did not think anything of it, just that he was in a wheelchair.

We found our chalet and settled into rest, eat and enjoy. We found out the chalet was the only one available as they were developing the site and there was a large crane in our eye-line. Undeterred and grateful, we decided we would enjoy ourselves anyway.

The following morning was a Sunday, and I awoke early to spend time with God before the day started. It was still dark as it was very early, around 4am. As I sat there, I suddenly received a (wait for it) DVD from the Lord.

God gave me a scripture, which I have never remembered since that day. He showed me walking up to the chalet behind us to pray for the man in the wheelchair. Yes, you have guessed it; our chalet was directly behind the one we passed earlier. I sat and watched as God showed me what to do. I saw myself going into the chalet, giving him the scripture, praying for him, and gently blowing on his face. God told me to first command the spirit of death off him and then blow new life into him.

I had never done anything like this before, so after asking the Lord when I should go and, making sure that it was indeed the Lord, I opened my eyes to find myself sitting on the veranda with my coffee in hand.

I cannot explain how I felt, doubting that I had heard correctly. After all, we were on holiday. I asked God, "What time should I go, Lord, as it is Sunday and they may want a lie-in?"

I immediately heard in my spirit, 8 o'clock.

Again, I asked Him if I could go at 8.30am, with the thought that they may want to lie-in late. To which God said a second time, "8 o'clock."

I started to cook breakfast and was keeping a close eye on the time; it was a minute to 8 o'clock when I served the eggs. Then came the first hurdle, I had to tell Ian. At that time, Ian was not in the same place he is now and would question my judgment by thinking, but we are on holiday! In those days, I found it harder to tell Ian than to be obedient. All things aside, I went up to the chalet, speaking to God all the way, asking Him for favour and acceptance. I did not know these people and did not know if they would chase me away or even allow me to pray for this man.

As I approached the front of the house, there was a young couple there and, as I did not know how to approach them, I asked God for a word. I then asked them sheepishly if there was a man in a wheelchair, to which they answered. yes. I asked if I could maybe speak to him. I found out later that the girl was his daughter. She shouted so loud for her mum that I almost jumped out of my skin. Her mum came out and after introduced myself and tried to explain somewhat haphazardly, I eventually said to her, "Let me just say it out loud. I believe God has asked me to come to pray for your husband!" What she did next really surprised me, she grabbed hold of my hand with tears running down her face took me into the chalet to where her husband was lying in bed.

She explained to her husband that I had been sent to pray for him and then introduced me. This man had an oxygen mask over his face with a tank beside the bed. He was not a good colour, and his skin had a greyish tinge to it. He was very poorly. I asked him if I could pray for him and told him what God had shown me early that morning. I also gave him the scripture, which he acknowledged heartily. He knew in his heart that God had sent me, and I was so relieved.

I prayed for him and did everything that God had shown, or so I thought. He was smiling and sitting more upright in the bed as if a great weight had been lifted off him. His wife, too, was smiling from ear to ear. It was such an honour to be part of their life story, even just to pray for them. As I started towards the door, the Holy Spirit stopped me, said, "You forgot something", and reminded me that I had not blown on this man's face. I turned around and said that I had forgotten to do something and asked if I could remove his mask for a second and blow on his face. He was very happy for me to do it, but I was not expecting what happened next. As I blew on his face, his skin seemed to turn a different colour, more pink than grey. I had finished my assignment and I was so blessed to have met these beautiful people.

As I was leaving, God had another surprise that I was not expecting.

The woman said to me, "You will never know what you have done today" I replied that I was only doing what God had asked me to do. She then floored me with this statement by telling me, "My husband has been diagnosed with a terminal illness, and this holiday will be the last one together as a family, and (wait for it) 'this is the only chalet in the entire Drakensberg that we could book for this weekend." We were both crying and thanking God for His goodness; we hugged as we said our goodbyes but I knew that God had done something amazing.

We left the following Sunday and as I looked up at the chalet, the man was sitting up in bed, waving through the window to us. What a beautiful sight to behold.

Thank You, Father God, Lord Jesus and Holy Spirit. All glory power and honour belong to You.

If you ask me why God chose me, I would say, "I know the answer! - I do not have a clue." I could try to think of possible reasons, but I do not have a clue.

I believe that just as Jesus performed all His miracles to bring God glory, so He does the same with us, not for us to be praised but to show Himself as compassionate, loving and good.

I do not know why some people are healed and others not. That is not for me to question, that is God's business and I am sure one day He will show us. All I know is that it is a privilege to work with Him and see His hand upon people's lives, changing their lives and their perception of who He is and that He loves them.

It is not about the power but about our relationship with Him and His Holy Spirit. The Holy Spirit is our best friend and as we stay close to Him, and submit to Him, He will do the work through us. He should be the first person we say good morning to and the last person we speak to at night.

CHAPTER FIVE | **New Seasons**

As we walk with God, just as the seasons of the year change, so does our spiritual season change although it might not be in the same time span as the summer, winter seasons. God wants to take us to the next level and, as we grow and learn, He teaches us in different ways. Whenever He starts to speak to me in different ways, I keep checking to make sure that He is in it.

Lately God has started to speak to me through dreams and, when I woke up, He would give me the interpretation, but not always immediately. What I did though was always to write it down. The Holy Spirit led me to Habakkuk 2:2-3 Then Adonai answered me; he said, "Write down the vision clearly on tablets, so that even a runner can read it. For the vision is meant for its appointed time; it speaks of the end, and it does not lie. It may take a while, but wait for it; it will surely come, it will not delay

God says clearly to write down the vision and I believe that dreams can sometimes be visions of the night as the bible calls them.

I have had some amazing dreams, some showing me to go and speak healing and others concerning the future that God has for me. They usually come with a scripture and sometimes I really do not understand what He is trying to show me.

Sometimes He may even give other people dreams that are part of your story. They might not be sure what God is saying but when He turns up as He did in this one instance, it is absolutely gobsmacking.

So, let me share this story.

I had been reading a biography of Katherine Kuhlman[1] and near the end of the book, she had said to the Lord, "I want to be your water carrier!"

As I read this, the Holy Spirit touched me and I said, "Lord, I want to be your water carrier."

I cannot say that I felt anything. All I did was to declare, Lord, I want to be your water carrier. A few weeks later, we held an annual conference at our church, amalgamated with WILLOW CREEK. We were one of the host churches.

As we sat preparing in prayer for everything to go well, the Holy Spirit prompted me to share what was on my heart. I cannot remember what I shared but as I shared, the woman next to me was getting more and more excited.

When I finished, she spoke to me and said, that she had a dream but had not known what it was about until I spoke. In the dream, she saw a woman from the music ministry carrying a yoke with broken, cracked pots at each end. Although she kept trying to fill them with water, she could not. She never looked behind her to see all the beautiful flowers that had grown as the water spilled onto the ground.

"Sue I know now that woman was you. God has shown me that you are His water carrier." She went on to say that even though I thought that I am not good enough to carry the water, and the pots are not whole, the attitude is right.

She looked at me as she spoke and said, "I didn't know who the woman was, all I knew was that she was in the music ministry. Now I know that it is you."

---

[1] Hinn, Benny, <u>Kathryn Kuhlman: Her Spiritual Legacy and the Impact on my Life</u>, W Pub Group, 1999, USA

I was so surprised and with tears streaming down my face, in amongst the hugs, I said, "Lord, it is a privilege to be Your water carrier. Help me to be humble and never take it for granted."

On another occasion, I had a dream. I think it was a dream or vision but I do not really know. What l do know is that, as I write this, I still remember it so clearly that I have to include it.

I dreamed I was on a plane to Guatemala. I do not know why there, maybe because of the high mountains. The plane inside was not the usual layout. It had a shower at the front where the TV usually stands. Everyone on the plane had a shower before landing, but each time I stepped into the shower, a man came and would not leave the area, so I did not shower. The man was very upset at that. In the next part of the vision, we were in a hotel lobby and the same man was complaining that I had not taken a shower. I asked him not to worry, as I did not think it a problem.

Then I was walking up the side of a very steep hill and passed by a house with crocheted curtains. I remember thinking that the people were so poor that this was all they had to put up; mind you, they were pretty. I remember crocheting squares in my youth to make a blanket. There was somebody holding my hand but I could not see who it was and as we walked up the hill, a woman coming down said to me, "There is still a way to go!" I do not remember my response, but I think it may have been, "No problem."

I looked over to my right side and looked down onto a beautiful lake. The water was clear and sparkling in the sunlight. There were a few youngsters diving into the water, having lots of fun. As I walked on up towards the top of the mountain, I suddenly became aware of three steps on the side of the mountain ahead. I do not know how I managed to get from one to the next, all I know is that I did, and found myself sitting on some steps in front of a small wooden chalet, much like a Wendy house, which is much like a garden shed, only better.

As I sat there, for some reason I was holding out my hands and as I did, oil started to pour from what seemed to be the sky. It just kept pouring and pouring, gallons and gallons of oil. When I finally opened my eyes, the oil stopped.

I opened my eyes and I felt as if I was waking up yet it did not feel as if I had been asleep.

God started to interpret the dream. He reminded me of Mary when she was told by the angel that she would conceive through the Holy Spirit, she cherished it in her heart. Likewise, I should cherish the vision of the oil upon my hands until I could share it with others.

As the year went on, God kept working in me and through me, teaching me to hear His voice and to be obedient to Him.

Visions are how we see what God has in His heart for us, our family, our ministry, but it does not happen overnight. It happens in His timing and in His way. Our job is to trust and wait. For most of us, waiting does not come easy.

We receive from God by faith, because without faith it is impossible to please God. (Hebrews 6:1)

Waiting also is not easy as we live in a microwave, instant world, but that is not God's way. He is teaching us all the time to be patient, to wait on Him and not run ahead of Him or even try to help Him; He does not need our help.

The next months seemed to be very uneventful, but I always remember my pastor saying, "When it looks like God is doing nothing, that is when He does His best work." God wants us to trust Him even when we do not see anything happening, we are reminded that we walk by faith, not by sight.

I have found that when I need encouragement and am starting to doubt, then suddenly, God will move and bring a scripture to mind to encourage, and strengthen me. Therefore, it was as I sat with Him one day, Revelation 3:7-8 and 10-12 came to mind.

7"To the angel of the Messianic Community in Philadelphia, write: 'Here is the message of HaKadosh, the True One, the one who has the key of David, who, if he opens something, no one else can shut it, and if he closes something, no one else can open it.8"I know what you are doing. Look, I have put in front of you an open door, and no one can shut it. I know that you have but little power, yet you have obeyed my message and have not disowned me.

10 Because you did obey my message about persevering, I will keep you from the time of trial coming upon the whole world to put the people living on earth to the test. 11I am coming soon; hold on to what you have, so that no one will take away your crown. 12I will make him who wins the victory a pillar in the Temple of my God and he will never leave it. Also I will write on him the name of my God and the name of my God's city, the new Yerushalayim coming down out of heaven from my God, and my own new name.

As you read these scriptures, listen to what the Holy Spirit is saying to you.

Keep on; keeping on, knowing that God is with you, He will never leave you or forsake you, He has never failed you yet… Whoever is reading this book, I believe you are not reading it by mistake but because God wants to speak to you through my words.

We are all unique yet God speaks to us individually. The amazing thing is that He knows how to speak to each one of us and how we relate to Him.

God has taught me many things from the numerous books I have read. The words seem to come alive as I read and I know God is speaking to me. This is something I have had to learn as I walk with Him. As I was reading one of my devotions, this came to mind: Go into the rain and get soaked to the skin. (The rain of the Holy Spirit.)

When we read the Word of God and read it alongside the Holy Spirit, it is as if we are being soaked in the rain. Do not put up an umbrella; just allow Him to soak you to the skin.

When He leads us through a storm, He will give us words of guidance. Our friendship needs to be deep, so deep, and our desire to follow Him and love Him, so great. When the time of difficulty is over, to be with Him will always mean to be shut in with Him.

In my prayer room, I have countless scriptures on the walls. I also have the lyrics of worship songs and words of encouragement that others have given to me. My prayer room is my sanctuary where I can be alone with God, worshipping, praying, listening and receiving from Him. I can be in there for as long as I choose whether it is for a short time or a longer time, but it is where I meet with God and break bread daily.

It is where God speaks to me and teaches me. For some reason, He has always referred to my heart as a garden, but maybe that is the way I understand Him better.

I often think about the parable of the sower and as I was pondering on what I was being taught, I reached the realisation that everything starts as seed. God gives us the word in seed form, and then it is our responsibility to receive it and plant it into the soil of our heart, just as we would in a physical garden.

What we tend to forget is that when we prepare our garden, all the weeds and such need to be taken out and the soil prepared for the seed. When it is ready, we plant the seed, water it and wait for the harvest. There are two growths that are necessary, the root going down and the shoot growing up. The root needs to be strong and go deep to sustain the shoots. The same goes for us, our roots must go deep in the love of Christ so that the fruit of the Holy Spirit can grow. Jesus is the vine, and we need to be rooted and grounded in Him and Him alone.

During my walk with the Lord, I have found that when He gives me a new word, then I am usually led by the Holy Spirit to go into a season of fasting, although the number of days vary. Over the years, I have learned that the first week is the preparation, which means weeding out the area that is overgrown. Imagine your garden; down in the corner somewhere is a patch of unsightly long grass. When you start preparing for a new bed, the soil needs to be dug up and the area weeded. The ground needs to be softened and fertilizer added to feed the new seeds so they grow strong and healthy.

Sometimes we forget that there is a preparation time when God gives us a word. When we do not see things happening, we tend to think that we did not hear correctly like Eve did in the Garden of Eden when the serpent tempted her by asking, did God really say? He wants us to learn from Him and to learn His ways. Yes, he can and does perform miracles when He wants to reveal Himself to us, but He wants us to draw closer to Him and learn His ways.

I believe that when God performs a miracle, the person receiving it has been crying out to God. We as witnesses do not know for how long, but God does, and so He sends us to pray for that person so He can do what only He can do.

Yes, God does it in His way and in His time but the preparation is most likely ongoing in the person's life. When we look at the life of Jesus and the man at the pool of Bethesda in John 5, he had been there for thirty-eight years waiting to be healed. Then one day, along came Jesus and healed him. I cannot imagine how he felt, although I know how I felt when God healed my leg. Amazed. We should never get out of the habit of being amazed by God.

As I think on these things, I am again reminded of God's goodness, mercy and grace.

I dreamed I was jumping higher and higher as if in slow motion. I woke up, but before I opened my eyes, I asked the Lord in my heart for the interpretation. I was led to Isaiah 58:13-14 If you hold back your foot on Shabbat from pursuing your own interests on My Holy Day, if you call Shabbat a delight, Adonai's Holy Day worth honouring, then honour it by not doing the usual things or pursuing your interests or speaking about them.

If you do, you will find delight in Adonai, and I will make you ride on the heights of the land and will feed you with the heritage of your ancestor Yaakov.

For the mouth of the Lord has spoken.

CHAPTER SIX | Going to the UK for Christmas

For a long time, I had dreamed and prayed about going back to England to fellowship with my daughter. Paula had married and left South Africa to start a new life back in her home country, the United Kingdom. I prayed that God would make a way for us to visit her, as we did not have the resources or finances to go.

One night I had a very vivid dream that somebody had bought Ian and me tickets to go and spend Christmas with Paula and her husband. In the dream, our pastor called us into her office and gave us the travel folder with the tickets and some extra spending money. Again, I remember coming out of her office and thanking God for His goodness. The date on the tickets were for the 17th of December which was the day before our anniversary. I was as excited as I woke up; I just knew it was from God. Therefore, I started to pray, thanked Him and started to prepare as we had a few months to Christmas.

I have learned since then that when God gives us revelation, the enemy will always come to deter us from the word given to us. It has taken me a long time to learn this. We were battling financially and I could not see how God was going to do this. When we look back at situations, only then we see God's hand. I had shared the dream with close friends, and they had assured me that God was in it, although I struggled to see this and my lovely husband certainly could not. (Bless him). However, I chose to keep believing and trusting.

Both our passports had expired and our holiday club annual fees were also overdue. I asked God initially for R2000 for passports but then needed to go back and ask for another R5000 to cover the annual fees. I believe that God is a God of multiplication and that He multiplies our offerings. He is a generous God, a God of abundance. I prayed for God to supply the R7000 to cover these expenses. I believe that God was testing my faith to see if I would stand on what He had shown me.

It was three months to Christmas, so I still had much praying, waiting, and trusting to do. As I waited, God led me to read a little book called, Hinds Feet on High Places.[2] It spoke loudly to me; I would, and have recommended it on more than one occasion.

Do you realise how hard it is to tell people that you will be with them for Christmas, but you do not know the flight number etc. because you are waiting on God? I think this was one of the hardest times of my life, although there is probably more to come. I see you smiling and thinking to yourselves, I can relate to that.

Then came a sudden breakthrough. I was relaying all this to a friend, Uri and had the distinct impression that God was busy speaking to him. I did not pry but left him in the office and left for lunch. It was my habit at that time to sit in my car and read God's word quietly with Him. Our staff canteen could get very rowdy during the breaks, so I opted to sit in my car. We were only allocated a half an hour's break and I wanted to use it appropriately. As I read, Uri came and crouched at the side of the car. He placed an envelope onto my bible, which I had propped up on the steering wheel. He told me a story of how he had been waiting for nearly seven years for God to instruct him where he should sow his tithe. He had recently completed an IT contract and was not touching the proceeds until God had instructed

---

[2] Hurnard, Hannah: Hinds Feet on High Places, Christian Literature Crusade, 1955

him where to plant the seed. While I had been speaking earlier, God told him, "This is where I want you to plant your seed."

I was surprised as he told me the story and wondered the amount in the envelope. I had asked God for an amount and then gone back a second time to ask for more, (like Oliver Twist) but I had learned to trust God. When I opened the envelope there was R7000, and I was absolutely amazed again at God's goodness and the obedience of a friend. Uri had left by this time, so I phoned him to thank him and to say how grateful I was. He told me the Lord spoke to him and that I had a calling on my life, and we should not let a passport hinder it. I was not expecting that, I did not see it coming and that makes it even more special and real. God answers prayer.

I am always so grateful to God that He answers our prayers, although sometimes He does not answer them the way in which we think He will, He answers them with what is best for us, and He uses people that are open to His leading and obedient to His voice.

Well, I hear you say, what if the person God touched is not obedient. That is another story.

God knew Uri well enough to ask him to sow R7000 into our lives to allow us to obtain passports and settle the holiday club fees. Sometimes when God speaks to His children, we question it, "Lord is that you? Do you really want me to do that?"

When God gave me the dream, it was my responsibility to receive it. When God spoke to the person to buy the tickets, I do not know what their response was (I cannot judge). Usually we only think about these things in hindsight. We cannot judge, we can only forgive, bless, and allow the Lord to do the rest. Believe me when I say it is not easy. We can start to question ourselves; wondering if God is really in this? I received multiple confirmations that God was indeed in it, so I kept praying thanking and trusting. When the 17th of December came, Ian asked, "What are we going to do?"

I replied, "We are going to the airport." Then I asked him to trust me, as this is what I believed God wanted us to do.

When we arrived at the airport with our luggage, I went around all the ticket windows to ask if there were tickets left for us. We only had enough money for a return ticket with the airport bus from Whiteriver, so we could not afford to go home until every prayer had been prayed and every last bit of faith had been used.

I checked all the flights and found that they closed at 8.30pm. One attendant reassured me saying, "Mrs Ralph, even if your ticket comes at the last minute, I will get you on the plane." Again, in hindsight, I believe God was testing our faith in Him but try telling that to your family who already think you are nuts. (Not easy)

I was trying to think how we are going to get home, as the last courier service was long gone. A friend had once said that if I was ever stuck in Johannesburg, then I should call her, so I did. We slept at her place that night and returned to Whiteriver the next day. I did not sleep much thinking how I must have got it so wrong. Next day I called Donne as she worked in a travel agency to ask if there was anything available on any of the airlines. Knowing in my heart that we did not have the funds and, of course, Christmas flights were so expensive. Suddenly she phoned me back and said there were two seats at a good price. My heart almost jumped out of my chest.

Still knowing that we did not have the funds, I cried out to God through the tears. I was probably complaining that I had trusted and believed. I did go on a while, although I did repent later. All I can say is that this is a testimony to His goodness and mercy.

We had only just arrived back home for half an hour when Ian said, "Don't, unpack the suitcases; we are going to the UK for Christmas!"

"How?"

He informed me that he was going to ask for a loan.

I was in shock at that moment, how were we going to get a loan? We could not afford to have more debt than we already had. How, would we pay it back? So many questions were running through my mind at 100 miles an hour.

I started to pray and give over all these thoughts to God. If it were not His will, the loan would not be granted. Within the hour, probably more like a half an hour. Ian was back and told me that the loan was approved and the funds would be in our account the following day. The flight was booked and Donne had confirmed the booking meaning the tickets needed to be paid by 1.00pm. The bank process took us right to the wire. The money was cleared and in our account around 12.45pm on the Sunday afternoon, just before closing time.

What happened to the tickets that had been shown me in my dream you may ask. I do not know. I do not know why, although much later, our worship leader had the revelation that the dream was from God and that He had been in control of all.

We had a lovely Christmas with our daughter and son in law and God made a way for us to pay the monthly instalments for the loan.

I again will add that this is my walk with Him, and this book is written to show His goodness, mercy, grace, and faithfulness.

CHAPTER SEVEN | **The Fast**

Every year, on the very first day, I ask the Lord to receive my fast as first fruits.

He very graciously accepts, and I ask Him, how I should fast. Usually it is a 21-day Daniel Fast of fruit and veggies and the occasional vegetable soup. Some years He has changed it to a 40-day fast. I reach to the end of the 21-days and He lays on my heart to go the extra mile, which to me means go through to 40-days.

I am always blessed when I fast. God strengthens me the whole time as I sit with Him daily and read His word. In previous years, I had been fasting, first for 3-days a week then the second half of the year for 2-days a week. I continually asked the Lord if He wanted me to do a 40-day fast but felt that I should carry on with this routine.

At the start of January 2009, in the UK, I did as I usually did and started my 21-day fast. My youngest brother had offered to take us to the airport to fly back to South Africa. We had a lovely time visiting Paula and our extended family that we had not seen for a long time. It was great to catch up with them. Our flight was on the 12th January; we arrived in good time, checked in our luggage and went for lunch. My brother is a generous person and knowing we enjoyed fast food, decided to buy us all beef burger and chips. I was so caught up in the excitement of us all being together that I did not think about lunch. As I bit into the burger, a sudden thought came to mind! Lord forgive me I am fasting! I sat up in horror as I was really enjoying the food.

In my heart, I repented and asked forgiveness. However, I could not waste this food and dishonour my brother, who had been so generous.

I resolved to carry on with my fast as soon as we arrive back in South Africa. I felt very peaceful as I spoke to God in my heart and watched everyone laughing and eating their meal. It was a beautiful picture of family togetherness, even though we were leaving again.

When we arrived back at home and after all the presents had been handed out and all the gestures of thanks the friends that had been house sitting finally left. It was nice to be home again, but we now had to go grocery shopping. In the shopping mall, I found myself going in the opposite direction to the supermarket as if I was on autopilot. I found myself in my favourite Christian bookshop. Wondering why I was there, I browsed until I came across a book on fasting by Jentzen Franklin.[3] , I asked the Lord one more time "Lord, when should I do a 40-day fast?

He answered, "Monday."

It was the most incredible time. I did not feel hungry for the entire 40-days. I allowed myself one cup of tea in the morning, then juice and water through the day and a vegetable Cuppa Soup in the evening when I cooked for Ian.

I was reading the book of Matthew and God gave me a fresh revelation of Matthew 4:4.Man does not live by bread alone but by every word that comes forth from the mouth of God. He had been feeding me as I read His word and it was absolutely amazing.

The day I broke my fast, I thanked God for helping me to finish, and also for sustaining me through the 40-days. He responded with Isaiah

---

[3] Franklin, Jentzen, FASTING: Opening the Door to a Deeper, More Intimate, More Powerful Relationship with God, , Charisma House , 2008, USA

43:4. You are of great worth in My eyes, you are honoured, and I love you.

Thank you, PAPA, Lord Jesus and Holy Spirit.

Just as the bible is a narrative and collection of stories of people's lives, so this book is a narrative and collection of stories, of how God at different times and places has touched people's lives through their obedience to Him.

When we read in the book of Acts how the emissaries or apostles as we know them, waited as the Lord had instructed, then did what The Holy Spirit showed them, we, as His representatives, can do the same. If we are obedient to what the Holy Spirit shows, Jesus said that we would do the same things that He did. In this book, everything I have had the privilege of seeing and doing could only have been achieved by allowing the Holy Spirit to work through me. We are His vessels and, if we are available, He will use us to touch people's lives. I am always amazed at what He can and does do.

Someone once said we are the recipients of realising the greatness of God in the light of our lives. I totally agree that when we adore Him and have a relationship with Him, He transforms us to be and do His works for His glory, and to show Himself to be the God of all creation who loves us so very much.

CHAPTER EIGHT | **New Direction**

Since learning to hear from God, I have been very conscious of the way I dream. As mentioned previously, I dream often, but not every night or rather not always vividly.

In this one dream, I was with a friend, EL, from church. We were walking through an orchard carrying gardening tools. There was somebody else in the orchard picking fruit and I turned to EL and said, "EL, this year is going to be an awesome year bearing loads more fruit." We came to a big tree that had been pruned back to within an inch of its life with only a few branches left at the top.

EL remarked, "Oh shame, look at that poor tree, it is been pruned so much."

I explained, "Do you know what happens when a tree is pruned like that? It quickly sprouts new shoots and the plant is more visible, it makes the healing process easier and increases the fruit the following year."

I believe that God was showing me that our pruning had started and that Ian and I would be on a new path of healing.

Whenever we are in a desert period, God encourages us to listen for His voice, to be still and hear His voice, and to know and trust that He will never leave us or forsake us. Sometimes He sends others to speak His heart to us, and to give us His words of comfort so that we know He has not forgotten us. He sees us where we are. He watches over us and He is in the boat with us, just as Jesus was in the boat with His disciples. It is not quiet resignation but joyful acceptance and anticipation and love that enables us to carry on and follow Him.

Through all of this, I have learned to ask for the interpretation of the dreams. Some are dreams of warning, some prophetic dreams, and some dreams of encouragement.

I have also learned to pray and leave all these things to God who is the interpreter of all dreams. When Daniel was asked by the King to interpret his dream, Daniel said to him, no sage, exorcist, magician or astrologer can tell his majesty the secret he has asked about. But there is a God in heaven who unlocks mysteries, and He has revealed to the king what will happen. (Daniel 2:27-28) The same is true of us, when we have relationship with God, He also reveals things to those who love Him and are called for His purpose.

When God shows us these things, it is up to us to ask and pray and to receive His will for our lives. He says in His word that He does nothing unless He shows His prophets first. (Amos 3:7) Does that mean we are all prophets? No, but we can all prophesy. When we are sensitive to His voice, He will lead and guide us.

I had been given a prophecy that we would be moving back home to the United Kingdom. The date was 7th September 2008.

I shared this with our pastor and some other close friends. I started praying into it and kept listening for His instruction. I learned from this that God's timing is not the same as mine. We had a house to sell, but God had not said to sell it yet, so we carried on with our daily work. I kept all of this in my heart and did not even tell Ian, as I did not think it was the right time.

"Lord. if this is from You, then You should speak to Ian." I held many conversations with intercessors, friends and prayer ministers all who clearly confirmed this was from God.

It is very interesting that, whenever God gives a revelation or prophetic word, the enemy always comes and tries to deter us from it. He will trick us into thinking, Did God really say that, and until we learn to distinguish his voice from God's, we will get into trouble. We can become double minded and unstable as said in James1:7-8 Satan is a liar and the father of lies and doesn't want us to fulfil what God has for us.

While I pondered on this dream, a friend likened it to being pregnant. I spoke to God about this and said, "Lord, some babies are early and some late"

"My timing is always perfect!" He replied.

These scriptures came to mind as I sat, read, and listened for Him to speak:

Deuteronomy 28:1 If you listen closely to what Adonai your God says, observing and obeying all His commandments, which I am giving you today, He will raise you up and all the following blessings will be yours in abundance. Never forget what God has done, praise Him daily, not only for what He has done but for who He is.

My sword that the Lord gave me specifically is Psalm 27:13. I would have lost heart had I not believed that I would see the goodness of God in the land of the living. This is my sword that I often use when the enemy is trying to stop me moving forward in God's plan for my life.

God is good all the time, and all the time God is good.

CHAPTER NINE | Birth Days

I do not know if you are anything like me, but I tend to want God to move as soon as He has shown me something. I forget that a baby must be in the womb for nine months or forty weeks. In this age of fast food and fast everything, we tend to think that God is the same. Even though I have seen Him heal in seconds, I also realise that He wants us to learn from Him and His ways. As I waited for Him to show me the next step and kept asking (nagging), He was very patient. Mark 4:28 came to mind. That by itself the soil produces a crop - first the stalk - then the head - and finally the full grain in the head.

In this, I learned that there is a process of waiting. Just as we wait for a baby to be born, we need to wait.

God reminded me of this on my birthday a few years ago. I did not look any older (ahem) or even feel any older, but I knew that I was a year older. Likewise, I needed to trust that which I could not see or feel but know in my heart that what He has said would come to pass.

The birthing of the prophecy had started to unfold. I asked the Lord what was next. I felt that I had to start decluttering. It is amazing all the stuff we can accumulate over the years. We had been in our house for ten years at that time, so you can just imagine. The home-gym and walker were first on the list.

We had just started the process when a friend came to encourage us with a word from the Lord. It is beautiful when God speaks to us personally and when He sends someone to speak to us on His behalf, especially when there's no way they could have known.

She spoke over us. "God is about to give you another seed to birth. He's about to open the windows of heaven and pour out blessings that will be so great that you won't have room enough to receive it all."

When God restores us, He does it so that we are suddenly walking in the light and can hardly recall how dark our lives had been.

Once we move into the fullness of our appointment with God's destiny, then we do not have to think about our past any more. We do not have the inclination to dwell on our past.

In Philippians 3:13-14, Paul says, Brothers, I, for my part, do not think of myself as having yet gotten hold of it; but one thing I do: forgetting what is behind me and straining forward towards what lies ahead, I keep pursuing the goal to win the prize offered by God's upward calling in the Messiah Yeshua. And with all the former things out of our sight we find ourselves free and loosed to do and to be all the things that God has appointed for us, when we receive the word by faith and ask that You water it, then a harvest will grow to glorify You, Father God. Amen.

I include some scripture to contemplate and allow God to plant deep into our hearts.

    Isaiah 30:18-26
    Psalm 13
    Psalm 46
    Mark 4:21 & 32
    Psalm 23

Those who hear the word accept it and bear fruit, some thirty-fold, some sixty, some hundred.

As time went by and we were being encouraged by friends, we were given a word from one of the friends: Time is short for us and that we are not limited to one place. Another friend from church said that she felt such urgency in her spirit that we should prepare ourselves. Not really understanding then but what they had said was that we had to step out of the boat.

it is a phrase that we often hear: If you want to walk on water, you have to step out of the boat... I thought that I had until God gave me a picture of me standing with the boat around my waist and my legs poking through the bottom. It was such a funny sight I started to laugh. I apologised to the Lord for laughing but it was funny. Trying not to run ahead of God, we spoke to a friend who had her own estate agency and asked her to come, look at the house and put it up for sale. It needed a lick of paint and some TLC; we had been there for more or less nine years.

In that time, we had done some work on it but it still needed a freshening up. I was praying one morning and Joshua 1:7-11 sprang to mind. Prepare provisions for within three days you will cross over this Jordan to go into possess the land that the Lord God is giving you to possess. Act today on what you know God has said and God will assure your success carrying out His purpose.

When we take that step of faith, God seems to say, "OK, now I know that you are serious." He then takes us to the next step. My pastor used to say when God asks us to do something; He won't give us the next step until we have completed the first task He gave us.

A few days later, I walked into my prayer room and heard the Lord say clearly, "Take all your stuff off the walls!" My prayer room walls were covered in worship sheets, prayer sheets, and prophetic words. If I took them down then the walls would need to be painted. I expressed my concerns to the Lord and I grew very aware that He was asking me to do just that. So once again, Ian and I discussed how we should proceed. Our friend at church was an estate agent and was only too happy to help. She showed us what we needed to do and we set about the task of painting. Her husband also helped through his contracting company. They were both very generous with their time and provided paint and labourers to help finished the job.

We worked hard as we had a deadline to get the house on the market. It was not easy but God kept us strong through the battles, which sometimes were likened to Nehemiah building the walls. We were in a physical battle and a spiritual battle. Whenever we hit a bump, we would pray, give it to God and wait for Him to sort it out; and He always did. What a Mighty God we serve.

Christmas came and went with no sign of a buyer. Then came the attacks of did God really say? Through all of this, we kept holding on and doing the things that we knew had to be done. Waiting, praying, and preparing to move. We did not have a date to move so we just had to wait. We received numerous words of encouragement and, at one evening service, one of the leaders said, "This is what I believe God is saying to you! 'I am with you, I will lead you and guide you, you will hear a voice saying this is the way, walk in it. When you turn to the left or the right, you will hear My voice clearly and unmistakably, do not look back at the airport, do not worry about the how, and just obey when you hear My voice.'"

This was God confirming that, as we progressed and trusted Him to do what only He could do, He was in control, so what more could we ask.

In our time of waiting, the Lord had me pray for different people with all kinds of ailments.

On one occasion, I remember, I was praying for our local GP who was also a friend from church. His wife was his receptionist. When I arrived for my appointment, as I waited, the Lord told me that I should pray for him. I thought to myself, but Lord I'm here to see him for myself. Well, I shared this with his wife and asked if she would come in with me, as I needed to pray for her husband. Immediately she informed me that he was in a lot of pain with sciatica. After explaining everything to him, he allowed me to pray. Having undergone a neck and back operation myself, I knew just how debilitating this can be. How amazing is God that He even used my pain to get me there so I could pray for the GP? God will use whoever and whenever if we are available.

Our lives are in God's hands and we are like a bow and arrow that God aims at something we cannot see. He stretches and strains us until we cannot stretch any further, then releases us for His purpose and lets us fly like an eagle on the wind of His glory.

Suddenly, in March of 2010, things started to come together. We had buyers for the house, missionaries that had come to South Africa from Mozambique. They were renting a house nearby until they could find a house to buy. They walked into our house and the man said, "This is it! This is the house God showed me."

We were very happy that a Godly couple had been led to buy our house. We now needed to find somewhere to live as they had asked for occupational rent so they could move in ASAP. We had been looking for some time when a friend from church directed us to somebody she knew. God put all this together for us in such a short time; it was amazing how everything just fell into place.

All we needed now was the date to move, and where to live. As we prayed, God showed us the date, but that only I was to move. Ian was to stay behind for three months. Even though I thought everything was so straight forward, when I arrived back in the UK, it was not at all as I imagined.

I had to buy a car, which is something I had never done before. I had Ian's brother to help as I was staying with him and his wife. I did not know any of the makes or models of cars here in the UK and although they all seemed to be a good deal, none felt right. God had a plan. He led us to a beautiful Mazda, a name I recognised, as we had owned one in SA. I tell everyone that this is my gift from God, a car I knew with low mileage, one owner, and not a scratch on it – an absolute gift from the Lord. I bought it there and then, after phoning Ian in SA to confirm it with him.

Psalm 34:8 Taste and see that the Lord is good; blessed is the man who trusts in Him.

CHAPTER TEN | What's Next Lord

Since I arrived back in Wales, I had been spending a lot of time praying, waiting, and listening for the next step. I remember saying to the Lord, "So what's next, Lord? You have brought us back to the UK so what's next? What would You like us to do?"

As I sat pondering, I felt the Lord remind about a one-day course I had attended in Nelspruit in South Africa. I did not know much about the ministry, but I knew that God wanted me to be more equipped. As I typed Ellel Ministries into my laptop, I scrolled through the programmes and found a course called, Micronets and again after much prayer, decided this is the one I needed to do. It was quite a long drive to get there especially for me, as I had not driven for long periods. Normally Ian would drive, and he was still in South Africa.

I arrived safe and sound and tired after such a long trip but I slept well that night.

I met with some of the other people for breakfast the next morning and found out that two of them had been pastors in South Africa but now pastors churches in London.

Suddenly God gave one of then a picture of a slot machine winning the jackpot that said TIC- TAC-TOE. He looked at me and said, "Sue, this is for you! God is saying you are slap bang in the middle of His will for your life." I asked God for confirmation and again He was faithful to give it. What was such a surprise for me was that God had also spoken to somebody I shared a room with, that she was to pay for some of my tuition as I did NETS.

Isaiah 30:21 and you will hear a voice behind you saying this is the way, walk in it, when you turn to the left or to the right.

God was leading me deeper into His plan for my life and Ian's although at the time I didn't realise everything He was saying but I trusted that His hand was on it all.

God's guidance is clear and carries with it such assurance that we know what to do.

God had been speaking to me about doing NETS all through the Micronets course. I knew we had enough money to do part of the 1-year programme but not all of it.

NETS comprise of four 10-week modules plus two mission trips. Although I knew that He had said to do all four modules, I wondered about the finances. I started praying and giving this all to Him as I believe that when God gives us a plan, He will provide, which I must add, He did, amazingly stretching all the finances to do all that He had said.

I was so excited about what I was hearing, but then I asked God a question that only He could answer, "OK, Lord, so if I am going to do NETS, then what will Ian be doing?"

I picked up a slip of paper, which said that Pierrepont was looking for people to work on the maintenance team, and the Holy Spirit did a back flip in my stomach. On the last day of the course, we were all given a certificate and I shared with one of the leaders what God had been saying. As I did so, she said, "Bring him, we need him."

I replied that if we were meant to be here, then we will be, by God's appointment.

Ian arrived having received a phone call from Pierrepont asking him to come for an interview. All I know is that God had given a divine appointment, and this is where we now call home.

God does not seem to use the same strategy every time, but as we continue to wait on the Him; our minds are renewed by His word and the Holy Spirit. As we wait, we experience this knowledge and direction that He is showing us. Do not be afraid but be aware of stubbornness and trust God. He will bring it to pass in His time, in His way.

Do not scratch around looking for promises that have not been given by the Holy Spirit. The bible has many promises and when the Holy Spirit quickens them to our spirit, we know that God will fulfil that which He has said.

Presumption is a dangerous place to be.

Smith Wigglesworth said this: Not one word of His promise has ever failed.

All that I need He will be, all that I need till His face I see, all that I need through eternity, Jesus is all I need.

Amen to that, He is all we need.

I remember one time when I was sitting with the Lord, He reminded about my GPS. I thought, Lord, what that has to do with Your guidance. I was reading Joshua 1:7 only be strong and very bold in taking care to follow all the Torah which Moses My servant has ordered you to follow, do not turn from it either to the right or to the left, then you will succeed wherever you go.

As I read this, God spoke just like a GPS. When we are travelling in the right direction, the GPS does not speak, but as soon as it is time to change direction, and then it speaks and says to take the next exit.

This is true of God. When we spend time with Him, listen to Him, and pay attention to Him, He will lead and guide us. God's guidance is clear, and with it, comes such assurance that we know what we must do.

He speaks with authority and is prepared to confirm His word to us. If there is any dis-ease in our spirit even if it looks ever so right, let the peace of God be our judge.

There is nothing better than sitting with Him, being still and knowing He is God and has everything under His Mighty Hand. Learning to trust and listen for His voice in a way that He speaks to us individually.

CHAPTER ELEVEN | A Brand New Season and New Year

Over the years, I have learned that September-October is the Jewish new year. It is always been on my heart to go to Israel and walk where Jesus walked. I have said to Him on more than one occasion that, "One day I will go there and walk where You have walked, Lord."

God had graciously given me a vision a few years before. I was having breakfast on the beach with Jesus. This had given me such a desire to visit Israel and I often prayed that one day I would be there. I was speaking to a fellow student who lived in Haifa in Israel and she had offered me an open invitation that when I came to visit, Ian and I should stay with her as she had an apartment at the top of Mount Carmel. I thought about it long and often; it would need to be a miracle from God as our finances were stretched at that time, but that is something I will tell you about later.

I awoke one morning having had a dream of a baby girl around 10-months old. Her father had died and her inheritance was being given away to other people. Suddenly they realised she was the daughter of the deceased and immediately started collecting everything that had been given away.

The interpretation was revealed to me as I woke up. The child was me and God was giving me back my inheritance as I now belonged to Him. The word of God came to my mind, John 10:10. The thief comes only to kill, steal, and destroy, I have come so that they may have life, life in its, fullest measure.

During the year that I was studying the NETS programme, God did a large number of healings in many different ways. As I learned how to minister, I was amazed at how diversely Jesus used me for His glory. Time was passing so quickly and, before I knew it, it was the end of November. The weather was cold, especially for my husband and me, as it was the first time for twenty-six years that we had experienced a cold winter.

One morning, as I sat quietly in our room, God showed me that I should undertake a Joshua Walk around the perimeters of Pierrepont. I saw myself walking in snow up to my knees. I remember thinking, well Lord, I do not know if that's just my imagination as there's no snow about yet.

I started the walk the next morning and as the week went on, there was still no snow. On the third day, I looked out of my window and, Lo and behold, it had snowed overnight - deep snow. I sat and spoke to the Lord about the snow. "OK, Lord, so it was You!"

I could not believe my eyes just how much snow had fallen. I did not have any snow boots, so I carried on with my Joshua Walk in normal trainers. It was winter; the nights were long and dark from around 5.30pm. I needed to walk the perimeter and parts of the walk were very dark, especially along the river path. I had two large torches and a lamp so that I could see where was going.

The first few nights, I had Ian accompany me along with an Australian couple, Greg and Sandra. We had met them on one of the NETS courses (I think it was stage 4). They also invited us to a local church on the Sunday. Sunday turned out to be the last day of my Joshua Walk, so I tried to negotiate with God to complete it the following day. It was like a wrestling match between God and I, for me to do what I knew in my heart was right. I had to walk the seventh time on the 7th day and not the 8th day.

As you can imagine, God won. I surrendered and walked the last day alone. I had battled with the thoughts of going to church but then decided it would be better for Ian to go with Greg and Sandra, as I needed to finish what God had asked me to do. The last day was extremely tiring as I walked and praised and shouted. God also told me to blow my shofar in the four corners of the grounds.

I needed to ask the Lord to give me strength to finish the last day, as the seven times around the boundaries was quite difficult to do in the snow and cold. My calves were sore and stiff with the cold. My trainers were wet through and by the end of the last lap; I could not feel my feet or legs. I do not know why God asked me to do this, but I was obedient and I'm sure He had a plan. It took me around 4½ hour's altogether but I praise God that I finished.

I went straight home to a hot shower and fell into bed. I prayed, "Lord, please touch my legs as I sleep and bring restoration so I can walk in the morning." I woke up the next morning early to find He is faithful; my legs did not ache at all. Praise God that He did what I asked Him to do. This scripture came to mind as I sat with Him.

Esther 4:14. And who knows but that you have come for such a time as this. For this occasion, I felt this was very apt for what I had just finished. Thank You ABBA, Lord Jesus, and Holy Spirit.

CHAPTER TWELVE | Spending Time with Jesus

I have learned over the years of the importance of spending time with Jesus. I just love sitting with Him in the morning, cup of tea in hand and sensing His presence. For me it is always the best part of my day even if it is not for as long as I would like. To sit and talk with the Lord as I would an old friend, sharing my thoughts, hopes and dreams, and listening for His response. I was now busy with stage 3 of NETS.

This day we held a day called, Spending Time with Jesus. We read a passage of scripture and then ask Him what He wants to say to us through it.

As I sat, I heard in my spirit:
Be still and know that I am God!
You are blessed because I have called you by name.
I will provide for all your needs.
I will keep you in the palm of My Hand.
Would I send you and not provide?
Is My Hand too short?

> As a father provides for his children, so I will provide for you!
> Keep your eyes on Me; keep your heart open to hear My voice.

I was then led to Isaiah 53; the entire chapter addresses us directly saying, the atonement has been made!

We do not need to do anything since Jesus has done it all on the cross. I, for one, am so very grateful. We just need to believe. Jesus Himself said that our work is to BELIEVE.

Thank you, Father, that You help us even when we can't believe. Thank you that You hear our prayers and put our tears in a bottle.

Andrew Murray once said (I do not know where), I have learned how indispensable it is to meet with God every morning in prayer and allow Him to take charge of my life for the day.

My prayer is, Lord that You meet with me as I sit with You. Take charge of my life every day. Thank You that You watch over me and keep me safe; that You will never leave me nor forsake me, and as I try to get my head around writing this book, that You will lead and guide me.

Thank You for Isaiah 40:31 But those who wait on the Lord shall renew their strength, they shall mount up with wings like eagles, they shall run and not be weary, they shall walk and not faint.

Over the years, this has been a key verse in my walk with God. He has often encouraged me with it.

I had been helping my team making beds etc. in between the stages of NETS, and was on the last break before stage 4. I had prayed many times and was trusting God for the provision to complete the last stage.

Pierrepont had awarded me a certificate at the end of stage 3 just in case the funds did not come. I received it in my hand but not my heart, as I knew what God had told me.

The Lord had commissioned my mentor and me to pray for Pierrepont every Monday morning. As we were praying, I asked her and another person that was with us to keep me in their prayers for the provision.

She immediately said, "It is done," and as I agreed with her, she said a second time, "It is already done." The next morning, I was approached by a team member that worked in the office and she was very excited to tell me the miracle that someone had donated the full amount for my stage four NETS. There was also exactly enough left over for me to go on the mini-mission trip to the Ellel Baak Centre in Holland.

I praised and thanked God once again, for His provision.

I have learned to have a grateful heart no matter how the day goes and no matter how I feel. There is always somebody much worse off than I.

You are EL-SHADDAI, THE ALMIGHTY ONE, OUR PROVIDER.

I love the scripture in Matthew 6:33-34 But seek first the Kingdom of God and His righteousness and all these things shall be added to you. Therefore, do not worry about tomorrow, for tomorrow will worry about its own things. Sufficient for the day is its own trouble.

I also love Psalm 100: 4-5 Enter into His gates with thanksgiving, and His courts with praise. Be thankful to Him and bless His Holy Name. His mercy is everlasting, and His truth endures to all generations.

CHAPTER THIRTEEN | My Testimony

As I was reading my devotion this morning, I read of how in Acts, Paul and Silas were singing praises to God whilst in prison. Suddenly there was what seemed like an earthquake and the prison foundations shook violently. The jailer ran in, began to tremble, and fell in front of them. (See Acts 16) For me this shows the power of God in action. The earth trembled but the jailer knew in his heart that there was an unseen power at work through Paul and Silas and asked how he could be saved.

Sometimes, when I must deliver a message or word from God to whomsoever, I tremble under the anointing. My legs tremble and so does my voice, as the Holy Spirit backs up the words He has given me to speak.

I am so glad that I know God has taken me out of darkness and brought me into His glorious Light. He has taught me to keep my eyes on Him, and give everything to Him, to capture my thoughts and also give Him any worries I may have.

God's word is powerful and true and sharper than any two-edged sword. It is alive and active and if we believe and keep believing, watching, and waiting, we will see the fruit of our testimony come forth.

When we have a relationship with the Father, Son and Holy Spirit, and we have a grateful heart, God will go out of His way to bless us. Actually, He says that we are blessed to be a blessing.

God picked me up, turned me around and inside out – well, that's what it felt like. God blesses us with daily blessings and benefits that sometimes we forget about. When was the last time you spoke to God and just said, Thank you, Lord? I pray daily to thank Him that He has made us to be a blessing in thought, word, and deed. I thank Him for trusting us to be a blessing to others in the way that He wants us to bless.

We are blessed to be a blessing. My pastor says we are the hosepipe that the water goes through to bless others, but in doing so, the hosepipe also gets wet. The blessings God gives us are not so that we can live a life of luxury but that we can give from the provision we have been blessed with, to others.

2 Corinthians 9:8 And God is able to bless you abundantly, so that in all things at all times, having all that you need, you will abound in every good work.

Lord God, I thank You that You have turned my life around, given me Your Holy Spirit to help me, to lead me, and to guide me.

I thank You that You have a blueprint for all our lives if we would just sit and listen to Your plan, the Divine Plan for our lives. We are called for a purpose, and God will bring it to pass, in His way and time.

You have the power that is greater than my history, and You can help me move beyond my circumstances to become the person You have designed me to be.

As I prayed, asking God, "What's next, Lord, as I am coming to the end of NETS 4?" I heard in my spirit, house, and prayer ministry. I thanked Him and asked for a confirmation that I had heard correctly. I kept it in my heart and waited.

A little while later in the week, one of the leaders approached me in the coffee lounge and said, "So I take it that you are not leaving, as Ian has not resigned. We would like to offer you a position at Pierrepont on the House Team. We do not want you to be just on the team but to run the House as the House Manager."

I was not expecting the last part but God did say I would be on the house team. I spoke to Ian and then accepted the position. It was quite hard in the beginning but I had worked in management previously and it improved as I found my feet.

I was doing well until I was seconded onto the Events Team. We had an event coming up and as I organised everything, I was pleased that everything was going so well. What I did not know was that the enemy was not happy at my appointment. The next day, the day of the event, called JESUS HEALS TODAY, was, to put it simply, a total disaster. Everything that could go wrong went wrong.

My friends had come to pray for people as part of the Ministry Team and John said to me, "Sue, this is your first event as the House Manager and the enemy wants to beat you down. But God is lifting up a banner to protect you." Times like these are exactly when we need to be aware of the enemy's tactics and I had to learn them very quickly. It was a very challenging day but after I had received some prayers, the peace of God came over me and the day improved by the minute. God is our Defender, Provider, and Saviour and so much more. When we stop to think, He is our all in all. I have learned to appreciate this fully and I am grateful for all the teaching.

Thank You Lord God, Lord Jesus, Holy Spirit.

CHAPTER FOURTEEN | First Fruits Fasting

As previously mentioned, at the beginning of every new year I ask God to accept a first fruits fast, and this year is no different. God has always referred to my heart as a garden and we all know that when a garden needs weeding, it can be an extensive task.

My days of fasting are like a garden being prepared. First, the earth has to be dug up and softened to make way for the new seeds to be planted and grow.

It is not easy or pleasant when some of those roots come out; things that have been there for a long time, but God is a good dad and knows exactly how to get them out. Of course, it is all about repentance and surrender and forgiveness, but He is gentle and compassionate as He sets us free.

I love the prayer that I came across recited by Bill Hybels and attributed to his Third Grade teacher, Miss Van Soelen.

Oh! Give me Samuel's ears an open ear O Lord!

Alive and quick to hear, each whisper of thy word,

Like him to answer thy call and to obey Thee first of all.[4]

God asks in 1 Samuel 15:22-23, has the Lord as great delight in burnt offerings and sacrifices, as in obeying the voice of the Lord? Behold, to obey is better than sacrifice and to heed the fat of rams, 23for rebellion is as witchcraft and stubbornness is as iniquity and idolatry.

---

[4] Hybels, Bill, from <u>Does God still speak Today</u>, Wisdom of the Wounded podcasts, 2023

This was God's response to Saul from Samuel when he was disobedient. We, too, can at times be disobedient without even realising it, which is another reason for spending time listening and waiting on Him.

My prayer is that I would wait on You more, listen to You more and have a relationship with You closer than ever before. To trust You for all my provision, to say without a shadow of a doubt, my Dad has it covered!

To be one with You, the Lord Jesus, and Holy Spirit. To know that I know that when I pray for people, they have what they request of You.

I find the more time that I spend with God, the more I want. His presence is amazing as I sit and wait on Him. Sitting at Jesus feet is not something that comes naturally, as we think we should always be doing something.

I also thought that until one day God said, "I did not make you a human doing, I made you a human being." Over the past ten years I have learned to sit with Him daily, just sitting, not praying or talking but just listening and being. When I am ministering to somebody, I sometimes ask, "How is your quiet time with God?" I am always surprised at how much they do! I was also like that until I learned to sit and be still and listen.

Psalm 46:10 "Desist, and learn that I am God, supreme over the nations, supreme over the earth."

I remember my pastor saying, we have two ears and one mouth so we should be listening twice as much as we talk. How can we hear what God wants to say to us if we are continually talking? Yes, there is a time for all the disciplines, but we should make a time just to listen. Sometimes I go to God and say, "Lord, I have not come with a prayer list; I just want to be with You." Those times are so special, as are all the other times spent with Him, but these times seem to be different. For me I think it is because all my attention is on Him and nothing else.

I woke up early this morning and as I sat reading about the power of prayer, I was led to read about the Kingly anointing. What I realised is that David was anointed as King, Priest, and Prophet. The anointing of God does not depend on external qualifications but on who we are in relationship to God Himself. God does not look at the outside but at the heart. (1 Samuel 16:7)

At our team meeting this morning, we had to choose a picture and ask God to speak to us through it. My picture was of two people in a small boat on a beautiful lake. The mountains in the background were snow covered and looked wonderful as the sun shone on the pure white snow. The water was clear and as blue as blue can be. It reflected the people in the boat. There were lovely green fir trees on the mountain that looked idyllic above the water's edge. As I pondered and thought about the picture, I was drawn to the people's reflection in the water. As I looked at it closely, listening for God's response, I felt that He was saying that I reflect Him even though I do not see it myself.

Sometimes we do not see God working in us so it is nice when He speaks so profoundly to us but again, we must listen.

I have just finished reading a book in which the author says, God whispers to us to draw us closer to Him and I believe that to be true.

In our world of noise, noise, and more noise, how often do we just sit and do absolutely nothing; just be?

Can you imagine for one moment what your spouse would think if you always talked but never listened to them? We need to communicate to each other in more ways than talking all the time.

When we sit with the Lord, we become like the tree in Psalm 1.

Like a tree planted by rivers of water that brings forth fruit in season, whose leaf shall not wither and whatever he does shall prosper.

Why? Because we have been in God's presence. When we sit and listen for His voice, He gives us encouragement and direction.

A word we were not expecting was given to us by one of the leaders at our local church.

God says I see your faithful works in My house and even though others may walk past you, I see the things you do, I see your faithfulness in My house.

I do not know what God did at that time, but my heart was different, suddenly I felt different and started seeing myself as God sees me.

I had a paradigm shift. I started to speak differently, especially to myself.

Jeremiah 23:29 Is not My word like fire? says the Lord, and a hammer that breaks the rocks in pieces?

Bring every thought into captivity unto Christ.

Look for Christ when you need a word of encouragement.

Allow the Holy Spirit to clean the mind through the reading of the word, the fresh living water.

CHAPTER FIFTEEN | **Being Ready to Hear and to Do**

God always seems to amaze me, particularly when we are on holiday.

On a few occasions, He has touched my heart to pray for somebody that I meet when we are away, and this time was no different. We were on holiday in Scotland and many friends thought it would not be special if we did not take a boat trip across Loch Ness.

The weather was lovely and I remember saying to Ian that we just had to go onto Loch Ness while we were there as, who knows, we may never be there again. I like doing the touristy stuff and even though I'm not really a boat person, I would brave it just to be able to say that I have been on Loch Ness.

I love it when the Lord prompts me by His Holy Spirit to pray for somebody even though it is uncomfortable to approach someone I have never met, but it is great to see their reaction when asked, "Can I pray for you?"

I was watching a man on the boat. He looked very yellow and so I thought that he was sick. I found out later that it is not good to jump to conclusions. I approached his wife and asked if he was sick, to which she replied. "No, he's always so thin and he can eat and eat but does not put on weight." We both laughed and had a lovely conversation, but I still had a sense that I should pray for him. I then asked her if I could pray a blessing over him and she asked, "Are you a Christian?"

"Yes, and I feel God wants me to pray for him."

Suddenly she ran to the other side of the boat and called to the rest of her group to come and meet us. I did not realise that they were with a group, but everybody started to clap and shake my hand and thank us for the prayer of blessing for this couple.

They were so open and hugged us as if we had known them all our lives even though they could not speak any English and the woman interpreted for us.

We prayed the Aaronic Blessing over them and were all still laughing and singing to God as they left the boat. It was an amazing experience, a God appointment.

We do not know why God wanted us to pray for them, but I do know God is an amazing, faithful God and we just need to be obedient. I believe that this was a divine appointment, maybe He just wanted then to know that He has not forgotten them.

God taught me that when I sense His presence it is because He wants to show me something or to say something. Sometimes I do not understand everything but if I do not know, and then I pray in tongues and lift to the Lord whoever or whatever He is bringing to mind.

Later in the year, I had a vision or dream of which I am not completely sure except that it was God speaking to me. He was showing me standing in front of people in a congregation and, as I spoke, people were being healed. I believe that it was a prophetic dream as it has yet to happen.

A week later, on my birthday, I clearly heard the Lord say to me, "Take courage, it is I, do not be afraid."

Jeremiah 17:7-8 (NKJV) Blessed is the man who trusts in the Lord, and whose hope is in the Lord, for he shall be like a tree planted by the waters which spreads out its roots by the river and will not fear when heat comes, but it's leaf shall be green and will not be anxious in the year of drought, nor will cease bearing fruit.

That was an amazing birthday present, thank you, Lord.

I have come to realise that God is always speaking to us but we are not always ready to listen. Sometimes we miss it, but He perseveres until we get it.

This morning, a verse that is special for me, kept coming to mind.

Psalm 84:10 I would rather be a gatekeeper in the house of the Lord than dwell in the tents of the wicked.

It is something very close to my heart and that keeps me close to Him.

God has blessed us so much since we came back from South Africa. Again, this morning I had a dream of thousands of white envelopes coming through the air to me or through the post to me. I believe they contained love gifts or finances, either for our ministry or for us personally. God said we would always have more than enough for where we want to go. Also, that we need not worry, as He is our Provider, He will supply all our needs according to His riches and glory. (Philippians 4:19)

Since we arrived back in the UK, we have had so many lovely breaks and holiday every year and cannot thank God enough for all His blessings and provision. He is an amazing God and Dad.

The other Rhema word He gave us was Hebrews 6:13-15:

For when God made a promise to Abraham (me). Because He could swear by no- one greater, He swore by Himself saying, 'surely I will bless you and multiply you.' And after He had patiently endured, he obtained the promise.

As I wait patiently for You Lord, I know that You are a covenant-keeping God, and not a man that You should lie. (Numbers 23:19)

As for the rest of the year, it was a good year with two other divine appointments to pray for people, and as we come to end of another year, God has taught me so much.

He has taught me more of Him, his love, His grace, His patience and I know Him better and His ways.

I know Him more than just knowing about Him.

I also realise that when I cannot speak to anyone else, He is always ready to listen, and He has taught me more about listening too.

Our lives are like a series of stories all put together called life. We all have stories and each one is different. Not all stories are happy, but God is with us through that story.

Ecclesiastes 3 puts it like this, For everything there is a season, a right time for every intention under heaven. My pastor used to say, it is just a moment in time and this too, will pass, although some seasons are much longer than others, but when they are the longer variety, God is working a work in us that He could not do at any other time. He changes our hearts and prepares us for the next season.

My favourite times are when I just sit with Him and sense His presence, just being. Making room for Him in my heart; making more room for Him. I have just been listening to a song by Casting Crowns called Make Room[5]. It has amazing words and is so true.

---

[5] Making Room - Matt Maher/John Mark Hall - Essential Music Publishing 2017

Is there room in your heart
For God to write His story?

You can come as you are
But it may set you apart
When you make room in your heart
And trade your dreams for His glory

Sometimes we do not make enough room for Him in the hustle and bustle of life.

Make room in your heart for Him.

CHAPTER SIXTEEN | The Crossing Over

As I walk into a new year with God and find myself sitting with Him once again as is my usual practice, He gave me a picture of me putting my foot into a river. It is a beautiful day outside and this picture is gorgeous and His presence so tangible. Just as Joshua and the priests put their feet into to water to cross the river, I sensed that God was showing me to put my feet into the water. (See Joshua 1) I remember God saying, As I was with Moses, so I AM with you. (Joshua 1:5) He has been building my trust.

Today was one of those days. As I sat this morning thinking about His love, I saw a picture of me diving in the ocean, diving deeper and deeper but never reaching the bottom.

I felt that God say, "This is My love for you, never ending, so deep it is unfathomable."

Jeremiah 3:33 Call on Me and I will show you great and mighty things which you do not know.

Over the past months, He has been rooting me in His love and helping me to understand that my identity is not in what I do but in who I am and whose I am.

I am beginning to understand and realise that it does not matter what I do; that is just my function but it is not who I am.

I am a daughter of the Most High God.

I am a Princess and God calls me Hephzibah, so I am princess Hephzibah. The longer I walk with Him the more revelation I get.

As I went through the week, God also confirmed through a prayer minister that He has given me gifts that I have not even used yet.

I believe this was to confirm what He had said to me, "Your time has not yet come."

We need to be patient, waiting on God's timing as He builds character in us. This is not always easy but it is worth it. God knows what He is doing and does not need any help, although we do try to help Him.

We just need to be obedient and glorify Him when we accomplish even a simple task.

One of my favourite verses is Matthew 6:33 ...but seek first the Kingdom of God and His righteousness and all these things will be added unto you.

We have volunteered for the past two years here at Pierrepont and were hoping to have a holiday somehow. We had used up all the money from the sale of our house in South Africa but were sure that somehow God would provide.

Friends of ours had been asked if they knew of anyone that could use a small caravan and they knew exactly who to give it to. Yes, you've guessed it; it was us.

We took it, did some renovations of new curtains etc. and it was lovely to be able to get off base for a week. We had a few holidays in it and they were so good. What we did not know was that God had bigger plans than just holidays for us.

Unfortunately, during the winter months, water had seeped in and it became damp. Ian had to strip it back and repaint it before it would be good enough to use again. We would not be using it, but it was too good to scrap so Ian decided to advertise it on a website called Freecycle. Almost immediately, somebody called to ask if it was still available. He asked if we would hold it for him until he could get here to see it.

A week later, he came and said he would take it if he could come back in a few weeks as he was busy renovating a house in France and needed somewhere to sleep so the caravan would be ideal. What we did not know was that this was an answer to his prayers. He had been through many battles and God was showing him that He does indeed hear and answer prayers.

Now this lovely couple had a caravan to live in whilst renovating their new home in France.

All glory to the Lord God Almighty, God of heaven and earth.

Through all these things, I see God working and teaching us to trust Him as He is in control even when we cannot see it.

I love Exodus 14:13-14 Moses told the people, 'Don't be afraid. Just stand still and watch the Lord rescue you today. The Egyptians you see today will never be seen again. The Lord Himself will fight for you. Just stay calm.'

As I sat with the Lord this morning, today's devotional was headed, Stand Still and Stay Calm. How often do we try to help God when we are waiting for Him to move? All we need to do is exactly this, stand still and see the deliverance of the Lord. (NKJV)

When God is teaching us to listen for His voice and follow Him, He takes it one step at a time, and those steps are actual steps.

They are ascending steps. The more we walk the path, the closer we get to Him. God shows us one step at a time and as we obey Him, He will take us to the next step. We won't see the whole picture, but we can see the next step.

Romans 8:14 For as many as are led by the Spirit of God, are called the sons of God.

There are two reasons why we fail.

1) We do not do what He asks us to do, and

2) We do not do it in His timing.

God has a plan, and the plan is His and is always perfect as He says in Jeremiah 29:11 I know the plans I have for you. His plans are better than ours.

The Holy Spirit is the carrier of the plan and the provision is on the other side of our obedience. When we follow His plan, we always have success because He will bring it to pass. There's no point in the Holy Spirit living in us if we do not take time to listen.

He has a plan and the more of the Word we take in, the more of the plan we fulfil. When God calls us and shows us, the purpose He has for our lives, we need to make sure, it is from God first.

God is always faithful to confirm, and I cannot say enough that this is how God has led my husband and me along the path that He has for us. He has an individual plan for every one of us, but we need to listen. We all have a place in the body of Christ and when He shows us, our response should be, Yes, Lord.

My pastor always says we cannot say no and call Him Lord at the same time, then He is not Lord. If we have truly counted the cost, then our answer will be a resounding, Yes Lord.

CHAPTER SEVENTEEN | Celebrations for the Nations

We arrived late at night after a long 6-hour drive from home to Llanelli in South Wales. We had left later than anticipated as we were attending the wedding of friends, and we stayed as late as possible.

It all started when a friend, Judy, had asked me if was going to the Celebration for the Nations in Wales. I told her I had never heard of it. It pricked my curiosity, so I started to search on the internet.

I found out this event happens every year and that I could book a tent for the duration. I did not want to go alone, so I prayed and asked the Lord to help me find somebody to go with. Ian was doing the NETS programme for 10-weeks, so he was unable to come with me, but I really felt led to attend.

My friend, Jacinta and I had been training in the gym each morning and as we exercised, I felt to ask her if she would like to go with me to the event. I explained to her that it was a 9-day worship celebration and that there would be no speakers, just worshipping the Lord. Long story short, she prayed, said yes, and we left for a beautiful nine days together.

We arrived and needed to find somebody to direct us to our tent. We went to the main marquee and as we walked in, it felt as if we had stepped into the presence of God.

It was amazing. It took us a while to find the right person, but God's presence was so tangible that we found it hard to leave. We just dumped our bags in the tent and went back for the rest of the night.

The whole nine days were wonderful.

One morning, the Lord led the Leaders to undertake a Joshua Walk. We were 700+ people in all and everyone joined in the walk. God gave the direction and position of how He wanted everyone to move. He was filling us up with new wine and pouring rivers of living water over us; it really was a beautiful experience.

One morning, we volunteered to go into town to evangelise and to my surprise, God gave somebody a word for me. He said that I had been re-commissioned and brought back for a purpose. I had not spoken to many people, so I had not told anyone that I had come back to the UK from South Africa. I accepted this from God as confirmation that we were in the place.

One morning, as we had breakfast, we met a couple of people from South Korea. One of them said to me, "I have a word from God for you." It was hard for him to share. He lives in Korea with his wife and children but felt that God wanted him to be at the celebration. Obviously, I had never met him before, so I tried to put him at ease and said, "Just say what you were told to say."

He gave me the message and he was right, it was not easy for him, but it was not easy for me to hear either. It was a word of correction, but I knew that it was from God. There is far more to this story, but I was grateful to Matthew for his obedience as it changed my life and my marriage.

We had torrential rain for the next few days and as I sat in my car, I noticed Matthew leaving, pulling his wheelie suitcase behind him. I opened the car window to ask where he was going, to which he replied, "I have done what I was sent here to do, so now I am going home to my wife and family."

He knew the reason he had to be in Llanelli, but he did not know who the message was for until Jacinta and I met him at the breakfast table. As we started talking, God showed him that the message was for me.

God asked me to lay everything on the altar and devote myself to my husband, which I did for six months until God showed me that I was going through the eye of the needle. God said, "You cannot talk the talk unless you walk the walk."

It was a pretty hard time but God saw me through it and later shared with me that the enemy had been trying to break up our marriage.

One of the funnier things that happened was that my phone kept dialling 999 and the Cwmbran police then phoned asking if I needed help. It happened twice and as I shared this with Matthew and Jacinta, I realised that it related to the message Matthew had given me from God.

Assignment finished, Matthew left for South Korea and his lovely family, and I had a clear picture of his assignment. I love how God puts things together and it is only later down the road that we understand why.

I was so grateful not just to Matthew but also to a loving God that needed me to hear His heart for Ian and me and to set us free from the enemy's grasp. God had brought about total restoration in our marriage all we can say is, Thank You Lord.

I believe that every person that crosses our lives' paths are put there for a reason, either to change them or often, to change us.

This was certainly a word from God to change me. I had not even realised how I had neglected my husband, as all I wanted to do was please God and do whatever He asked me to do, This is not necessarily a bad thing, just that I was out of balance and this was enough for the Lord to correct me and set me back on the right path.

God had also shown me that I should buy Ian a new wedding ring as the one he was now wearing was not one that I had bought for him and there was a problem with it. Ian's wedding ring was a replacement from an insurance claim as he had lost his or rather it went missing from the bathroom and we never found out where it went.

What God had shown Ian was that it was a second-hand ring from somebody that had been divorced, not a new one as we originally were told. As Ian was doing NETS at that time and I was in Wales, we took it as confirmation of what God was saying. I had a picture in my mind of the ring that I should buy to replace it, and after saving enough money, we went shopping together. We looked in quite a few jewellery shops and eventually found the ring exactly as God had shown me.

It is now Ian's third wedding ring. The first was lost, the second was cursed and the third one was God's choice. The best part of this story is that I have also had three sets of rings. The first two rings had been stolen at different times, and then the third one was God's choice. When we looked in the jeweller's window, the Holy Spirit touched my heart, and I knew that was the one. To end this story, we have matching rings. The rings are white gold on the inside with a band of yellow gold around the outside. We could not have done better had we tried ourselves. We also received a beautiful blessing spoken over them and us by one of the leaders and I am so grateful to God for showing us all of this.

He shines His Light on Darkness even when we do not know it, He said, "Walk into the deep water, you are in the water, keep coming and I will embrace you, keep coming into the deep water."

Isaiah 41:10 Fear not for I am with you, be not dismayed for I am your God, I will strengthen you, yes, I will help you, I will uphold you with My Righteous Right Hand.

Leaving Llanelli, I wondered what this next season would look like. I was speaking to a guy, Oday, who I later learned was a pastor. He was busy sweeping the eating area and emptying the bins. He was busy talking about the time when he had been asked by God to lay everything on the altar. He was not speaking to me directly but I was close enough to hear what he was saying. I had to ask, "How did you feel?" It was quite clear that it had been a hard time for him as not only is he a pastor but a worship leader and missionary as well.

Oday's testimony really touched my heart, but I had questions! I asked him, "How did it feel when God said that to you?"

He replied that he felt terrible.

I also asked him, "How long did you need to lay it all down?"

His answer was, "Well, for me it was three months but it depends on how long God says to." He said he has known people that the laying down lasted for months or even years.

I had so many questions as I didn't understand how or why or what it meant to lay everything on the altar. All I knew is that his words had touched me deeply and I wondered if that is what God wanted me to do. When I arrived back home, I prayed, and I asked the Lord how He wanted me to do this.

As I prayed, I felt the Lord speak to my heart, He did not want me to minister to anyone or lead worship or do anything that I would normally be involved with. I had to devote myself to Ian, my husband and go about my normal work as housekeeper.

I spoke to my manager and shared what I believe the Lord had said, and he agreed that what I had heard was from God. As I did not know how long this was to last, I found myself saying to God "OK, Lord, as I go through this time, I will take it at face value that it will be for three months, but I put it on the altar and if it is longer then I know that You will show me."

I can honestly say that this was one of the hardest times I have ever gone through. I cannot describe how I felt but as Oday had said he felt terrible, so I, too, felt terrible. I felt as if I was being punished but I knew that was a lie. I tried to battle these feelings and kept asking the Lord to help me.

When I reached the end of the three months, I thought, Yes! I can start ministering and leading worship again. When I checked in with the Lord, however, He said, "I want you to go the extra mile." For me this meant go another three months.

My first reaction was, "Lord, what have I done that You punish me so!" Little did I know then or realise it was not punishment; rather that He was taking me up a level.

When God refines us, it can feel as if we are being punished, but it is learning to know Him and His ways.

A little while later, I was having a pity party with the Lord and a friend gave me a letter that she had been given on a Going through the Eye of the Needle course.

As I sat on the stairwell reading it, the tears were streaming down my face. I felt like the Lord was right there with me as I read. Have you ever read something, and the Lord shows up big time to the point that you sense His presence so tangibly as if He were standing right beside you? This was one of those times. I was sobbing as I read this letter; it was as if it was written just for me.

As I read the letter, everything was made clear to me as to why God had asked me to lay everything on the altar. I was not being punished; I was being promoted and humbled under His mighty hand. I was being prepared for a new season. I realised that God always has a plan and that again, it is walking the walk before I can talk the talk.

It was a lesson on humility and submission. I sat at Jesus feet daily and devoted myself to my husband until God said to go forward.

It was also an exercise that I had to relay to the team but first I had to understand and walk the path that God had for me.

I am also a lot closer to God through all of this and relying just on Him.

John 16:33 Jesus said,' in this world you will have trouble, but be of good cheer, I have overcome the world.'

When we humble ourselves under His mighty hand, He will raise us up.

Amen and amen.

CHAPTER EIGHTEEN | A Jubilee Year

A new year and a new season, and hopefully a better year than the last one. As I have said on more than a few occasions, every year I consecrate myself to the Lord with a 21-day Daniel fast.

I had just finished my fast and was led to follow a 40-day bible-reading plan. God has always referred to my heart as a garden and this reading plan was to sow new seeds for the coming year. The introduction period was a period of preparing the ground, just as you would prepare ground for planting; we need to prepare the ground of our hearts with the help of the Holy Spirit.

The next was the planting period and then, the tending of the garden.

Ephesians 3:14-15. For this reason, I bow my knee to the Father of our Lord Jesus Christ, from whom the whole family in heaven and earth are named.

Lord, I open my heart to You so that You cause these seed to grow healthy shoots, mature plants, and then into an abundant harvest of fruit in my life for You.

Ephesians 2:10 For we are His workmanship created in Christ Jesus for good works, which

God has prepared beforehand that we should walk in them.

In Luke 8, Jesus talks about the seeds that fall onto various types of ground. Verse 15 says that the ones that fell on good ground are those who, having heard the word with a noble and good heart, keep it and bear fruit with patience. I do not know about you, but I often find myself being impatient, wanting the seed to grow quickly.

I have recently been watching a pot plant sprouting a new flower and it has been such a slow process I cannot tell you. I have spoken to it, prayed over it, watered it, fed it, you name it I have done it. Did it make any difference? No, it did not. It was worse than watching paint dry, but it has flowered in its own time not mine and now I have a beautiful strong Lily, just the one but it was worth the wait. We need to be patient, and while we wait, God will carry out His work in us. Not easy, but worth it.

While God was preparing my heart, the little things that usually do not bug me, seemed to make me emotional and fed up. Going through the processes, I have come to realise that He is doing something in the garden of my heart although it took me some time to realise this.

I was reading the word and allowing Him to do His work when I suddenly started to think that I was somehow different. It had always been my heart's desire to visit Israel and to walk where Jesus had walked. I had been given multiple visions and dreams by God of being in Israel but with limited finances, I knew that we could only visit when God made the way for us to go.

I was busy chatting to a NETS trainee, Usha, one day and she said to me that when we visit Israel, we could stay with her at her apartment at the top of Mount Carmel. I thanked her and said it would be amazing but God would have to provide the resources and tell us when it was that He wanted us to go.

Ian and I were totally amazed to find a few days later that, unbeknown to us, God had been speaking to another NETS trainee, Martin, and had instructed him to pay our airfare. We had only to pray and let him know when. Martin gave me his phone number so that we could contact him with all the details as soon as we knew.

I kept thinking, October, and did not understand why, so eventually I typed into my laptop, what is on in Israel in October. To my surprise, I saw it was the Feast of Tabernacles!

Leviticus 23:24-32 (abridged) 24Tell the people of Israel, 'In the seventh month, the first of the month is to be for you a day of complete rest for remembering, a holy convocation announced with blasts on the shofar.

27"The tenth day of this seventh month is Yom-Kippur; you are to have a holy convocation, you are to deny yourselves, and you are to bring an offering made by fire to Adonai. 28 You are not to do any kind of work on that day, because it is Yom-Kippur, to make atonement for you before Adonai your God.

31...it is a permanent regulation through all your generations, no matter where you live.

32 ...you are to rest on your Shabbat from evening the ninth day of the month until the following evening."

It clicked very quickly that the date that had been jumping out at me was a reference to this scripture.

To make a very long story short, I changed my leave and God blessed us in Israel with somewhere to stay and paid flights along with spending money for the trip. We spent three beautiful weeks with Usha at Mount Carmel and even had a driver to show us the sights, and places that Jesus had walked. It was a time of great joy, the extravagance of God being and doing exceedingly abundantly more than we could ask or wish for. We were so blessed and able to see God at work as we prayed for people that He brought across our path.

God said, "You are precious in My sight little one. You are My treasured possession and I love you." He reminded me with a song that He makes a way where there seems to be no way. God also led a friend to bless us with a substantial amount of money sown into the trip. Another person gave me a beautiful new journal for the trip with a blue dragonfly on the cover. She did not know that I like blue dragonflies but had felt God say to her to buy it for me for our Israel trip. How amazing is God that He looks after all the small things as well as the large?

There are just so many highlights, unfortunately too many to write them all here. One of the best moments, however, was a simple encounter (God-ordained). We had arrived in Jerusalem for three days and checked-in to a hotel named, The Jerusalem Gold, situated directly over the bus station. The next morning, as we were having breakfast, the Holy Spirit touched my heart. I saw an old man hobbling along, trying not to put any weight onto his one foot. He looked to be in much pain. I went to ask him if I could pray for him but he did not understand English so I tried to sign it, showing him my hands together for prayer, but he still did not understand.

Eventually another member of his party came over and I explained to her that I would like to pray for him. She interpreted for him, and he smiled so wide. I prayed for him and left to finish my breakfast. The next morning, as we sat eating breakfast, he came into the dining room walking so much better. Praise God for His goodness.

We had worshipped with people in churches and had been touched so deeply that I said to the Lord that I could not have made this up even if I tried.

Thank you, PAPA, for an amazing trip to Israel.

Since we came back from Israel, I have been so blessed with the Lord's presence, even more than usual and it is such a privilege.

I have always wondered what it would be like to fly in a hot air balloon but never really pursued it; A friend suddenly gave me a ticket for a balloon ride. She said it was an early birthday present and as she would not be able to use it, she had prayed and thought of me. She also gave me a book that her friend had written, saying that it was a prophetic act ahead the book that I would write. I looked at her and thought, there is no way I am going to write a book. Well, how wrong was I on that count? This is the book that she prophesied I would write. I prayed so much into this as without Him, I can do nothing.

As we walk with God daily and spend time in His presence, He changes us and we become more like Him. When you think of the people with whom you spend time, they can sometimes rub off on us. Once we get to know them better, we know exactly what they will say or do in a situation. I believe that it is true of when we spend time with the Lord, He rubs off onto us and we become more like Jesus.

He is preparing our hearts for the things that He has for us, but we need to be patient and trust that God will bring things to pass in His own way and in His timing.

I was sitting with Him one morning, reminiscing on some of God's suddenlies.

When we are waiting on Him, trusting and praying for a situation to change, He suddenly steps into the boat with us and things seem to move quicker. It is not that He has not been there but suddenly our eyes are opened to what He has been doing. When I look back at my journals, He highlights things He has done, and now I can see the path He has taken me down.

Whatever we are going through, when we allow God to have the final word, we are in a better place. He knows what we need and when we need it.

Now, as I approached the end of another year, God gave me a final word.

Revelation 21:5 Then the One sitting on the throne said.' Look I am making everything new, and He said to me, it is done, I am the Alpha and the Omega, the beginning, and the end, I will give of the fountain of the water of life freely to him who thirsts. He who overcomes shall inherit all things and I will be his God and he shall be My son/daughter.

Father, thank you for all that You have done this year, for us and through us. It might not always be easy, but it is always worth it.

Bless You, Father God, Lord Jesus, and Holy Spirit.

Amen and amen.

CHAPTER NINETEEN | Behold, I will Do a New Thing

I have found that whenever God is doing a new thing, it is usually something I need to learn to walk in. I remember when a friend said to me, "Sue, remember when you ask God for patience, He does not just give patience or drop it onto you, He gives you more opportunities to be patient."

While we were in Israel, a friend, we met there gave us the same scripture but added that God's peace and health and rain of blessings would be upon both Ian and I, according to His plan for our lives.

I was reminded of this when I was in Wales. He said He will give me words to speak and they will come to pass, Psalm 81:10.

The Psalmist goes on to say that, the people would not heed His voice, and I guess that it is still the case today. The lesson is that my responsibility is just to deliver the message and leave the responsibility to the recipient(s) and the rest to God.

I needed to learn that I was not responsible for their response. The Lord said that when I speak and they reject the message, they are not rejecting me but that they are rejecting Him.

We need to know Him intimately. We need to know Him in every aspect, not just as Saviour but as Lord and Friend.

As we practice sitting in His presence, every day brings a fresh revelation of who He is. We need to know His gentleness and meekness.

The Lord said to me, "You have to know Me as the Lamb before you can know Me as the Lion."

As we sit with Him, He gives us understanding and revelation.

When God gives a word, then we should ask Him, "What do You want me to do with this, Lord? Is it for me or do you want me to pray into it? Is it for somebody else?" Sometimes when I get a word deep in my spirit, I will sense that it is for me to declare aloud! However, I always wait for the leading of the Holy Spirit.

Joel 3:16, Adonai will roar from Tziyon, he will thunder from Yerushalayim, the sky and the earth will shake.

Jeremiah 25:30 'Adonai is roaring from on high, raising his voice from his holy dwelling, roaring with might against his own habitation'

Amos 1:2 Adonai is roaring from Tziyon; thundering from Yerushalayim;

These verses all speak about the roar of the Lord from Zion. As I read these scriptures, I felt the Lord saying, "The Lion must roar in Wales, in Britain and establish victory. We are to be bold as a lion and we need to be grafted in very well to Israel."

Joshua 10:24 Your foot is on the neck of your enemy.

The roar must be in us, it is the power of the Kingdom in manifestation.

We know that we have the authority, and we know we are supposed to have it because Jesus said, Behold I give unto you authority. (Luke 10:19)

Let these words resound in your spirit. Let them strengthen you and empower you and pick you up from wherever you might be. Authority of the Gatekeeper- by Miriam Clifford[6] is a very powerful read.

I found this very easy to read and likened it to being the gatekeeper of my mind.

2 Corinthians 10:4 For the weapons of our warfare are not carnal but mighty in God for the pulling down of strongholds, casting down arguments and every high thing that exalts itself against the knowledge of God, bringing every thought into captivity to the obedience of Christ and being made ready to punish all disobedience when your obedience is fulfilled.

I believe God was teaching me to be the gatekeeper of my mind by not allowing junk into my mind but to quickly take authority and cover it with His precious blood. He has given us a free will and the ability to discern His purposes for us. He also gives us the opportunity to ask when we are not sure.

This is how we learn to know Him better.

When we read other people's stories, it is so easy to think that it is just for them. It is so easy to start to believe it will never happen for me. Well it won't if we keep comparing ourselves to others, but the word of God says that if we believe, that we have received them in prayer, it will be ours according to God's will. (Matthew 21:22)

When we stop and take time to be with the Lord and ask Him to show us what to pray, He will give us the words to pray according to His will.

Why don't you stop right now?

---

[6] Clifford, Miriam, S. GATEKEEPER, Xulon Press, 2011

Be still and listen!

Listen to what the Holy Spirit is saying right now!

What does God want to say to you right now?

What is your heart's desire?

Pray that prayer, the prayer that is not a safe prayer. He knows your heart, He knows the desires of your heart, the word of God says He gives us the desires of our heart. (Psalm 37:4)

Who put those desires in your heart to start with?

We all have stories to tell and God puts people in our lives with whom we can share stories. They are not always the same but similar to our story. God has made us unique, and our stories are unique, but He will use them to help others and to encourage others. We all start from the same point, salvation, and as we grow with God, He reveals Himself to us more.

It took me a long time to learn that just to sit with Him is the most important thing, to have a relationship with Him, not the gifts and talents or the singing but just Him. I have said to Him on more than one occasion, "Lord, when I get to heaven as long as You are there nothing else matters, no gold streets or mansions, just You."

Stop and think what that means for you right now; just You, Lord Jesus, just You. When ministering to people, I sometimes ask the question, "What is your quiet time like? How often do you sit with Him and say absolutely nothing but just sit?"

God taught me that a long time ago.

Psalm 46:10 Be still and know that I am God. Just sitting with Him and saying nothing and waiting for Him to come is hard for most people especially if we are always doing something, like Martha. Always thinking of what needs to be done next. (See Luke 10:38-42)

I was like that for a long time having worked as a retail manager for fifteen years, needing to think months ahead. I found it difficult to sit in one place for long.

The hardest thing for me when I did the NETS programme was sitting in one place for eight hours a day for ten weeks. It felt as if the Lord was saying, "Now you have to sit still."

He did great things in me, and I am so grateful for the time.

I did all four terms, and it became slightly easier as the year went on.

Let's get back to the story. I hope you had fun sitting with Him. I find that God does not say much in those times of sitting but being in His presence is so sweet. I do remember Him saying to me one time, "I did not make you a human doing; I made you a human being." I think we forget that we need to be like Mary sometimes, and daily just sit with Him.

As one of the leaders spoke this morning, I saw a picture in my mind of a two-bed roomed cottage. I did not see anything else so I gave it to God and said, "Lord I do not know when or how it will come but I trust in you."

Proverbs 3:5-6 Trust in the Lord with all your heart, lean not on your own understanding, in all your ways acknowledge Him and He will direct your paths.

This scripture came to mind along with the picture; so again, I thanked the Lord and gave it to Him.

The year, so far, seems to be a year of intercession and prayer, more than usual. As I have been praying, led by the Holy Spirit, I found myself praying over my children and grandchildren, friends, and family that are close and those that are far off, both physically and spiritually.

The main theme has been to pray for our children (all children), thanking God for them and speaking blessing over them.

From Mike Shreve's book, 65 Supernatural Promises of from God for your Child,[7] my personal prayer is Isaiah 49:25-26 (NKJV). He will contend with him that contends with thee and I will save thy children.

I believe this to be God's promise to me for my children as He has brought this to my mind on more than one occasion. Our children need to have a personal relationship with the Lord but we can speak blessings over them and thank the Lord that His hand is upon their lives. He will reveal Himself to them in His time and in His way.

Sometimes, we can think that because our children are not walking with Him like we are, God cannot bless them. The first line of Psalm 23 says The Lord is my shepherd.

One day, as I went for coffee with a friend, he asked me that question, "What is the first line of Psalm 23?"

"Corks! The Lord is my shepherd."

He then asked, "So who is Ian's shepherd?"

Again, I answered, "Corky, the Lord.

I did not expect what he said next, "Well that's good as God told me stop trying to do His job for Him."

The lessons were to pray and leave it for God what only God can do, otherwise we are trying to do it in the flesh, and it becomes a religious thing, doing this and that. I learned very quickly.

---

[7] Shreve, Mike: <u>65 Supernatural Promises of from God for your Child</u>, Charisma House, 2013

As time goes by and we walk with the Lord one day at a time, we understand Him more and start to know His ways. I tend to ask the Lord to forgive me when I do not learn quickly but He is always gracious and patient as we go through the process until we learn. Like being in school, we can't learn unless we keep trying until we understand, and then learn.

We often run ahead and, other times, we lag behind so keeping in time with God is important, one step and one day at a time.

It is a daily battle of choosing to walk with Him and to trust Him through it all.

We all have a story to tell and even though our stories are different, God's is always the same. He is the same yesterday, today, and forever. (Hebrews 13:8)

When we seek first the Kingdom of God and His righteousness, everything else will be added to our lives. (Matthew 6:33) He is a God that keeps His Word and His Covenant with us, and He does what He says He will do, but in His time and in His way.

Isaiah 55:8-9. For My thoughts are not your thoughts and My ways are not your ways, says the Lord, for as the heavens are higher than the earth, so are My ways higher than your ways and My thoughts higher than your thoughts.

CHAPTER TWENTY | **The Gatekeeper**

One of my favourite verses is Psalm 84:10 For a day in your courts is better than a thousand. I would rather be a gatekeeper in the house of my God, than dwell in the tents of the wicked.

This is something I repeat back to the Lord regularly, along with Psalm 100:4 I enter into your courts Lord with praise and thanksgiving.

I love these verses and often speak them back to the Lord For me it is in reverential awe and fear of the Lord.

This morning I was awoken with a dream. I love watching a BBC program called, Escape to the Country. I also had the song, Faith, in my heart. I have learned that when I dream so vividly, to pray, give it to the Lord and ask for the interpretation. If it is from God, then He will bring it into fruition.

In my dream, I was walking into a house to which somebody had given me the keys. I had met a friend and her children and as we sat in the lounge, I said to them, "From tomorrow this house is ours (Ian's and mine)". Somebody had given us the keys and the house is ours.

Two or three weeks later, we were approached by leadership and asked if we would move into the gatehouse, which is a lovely old cottage at the entrance of the property. The previous gatekeepers were being moved onto their next assignment and we would be anointed as the next gatekeepers if we would agree. We prayed and sensed that it was right. I also asked the Lord to give us confirmation that it was His plan for us.

He gave me a picture of a cottage with streams of light flowing out of all the windows and doors. I must be honest it was not where I expected it to be as I thought it would be back in Wales. Nevertheless, God is in control and if this is where He wants us, then that settles it, although I must admit that I said to God, "Well Lord, I got to the gate."

We moved into the Lodge and were prayed for, anointed, and ordained by the leader as the gatekeepers. We also did some cleansing of the property and its surroundings.

The next morning the entire area was covered in mist, which I view as God's glory cloud. It covered the whole grounds and was amazing to see. I also saw a mental picture of me being held in His arms and being hugged like a child. I then realised even more that, I am His child.

I had no idea what was expected of me as a gatekeeper, so I asked the Lord, "Lord, what does a gatekeeper do? Because I do not have a clue?

As I stood in front of the bay window, staring at the gate, He showed me a picture of a lighthouse on the edge of some rocks. I heard in my spirit: A lighthouse does not do anything but shine its light to deter ships from the rocks and so, you as the gatekeeper do not do anything but shine your light.

As we stay close to Him and live in Him, His light shines through us from the cottage and will deter the demonic.

Even after all of this, I still sought God for confirmation as I had come under attack with stomach trouble, vomiting, cramps and fever. I found myself in bed for an entire day and spent it rebuking the illness, speaking God's truth over myself and declaring that the enemy would not prevail, as God is my shield. Ian prayed for me, and I had peace for the rest of the day. As mentioned, Psalm 84:10 is one of my favourite verses and I often quoted it back to God. For a day in your courts is better than a thousand. I would rather be a gatekeeper in the house of my God, than dwell in the tents of the wicked.

Speaking to a friend, she said, "Sue, as I was walking around the little pond, I had the urge to take a picture of this gate, but I did not know why!" When she sent it to me, I knew exactly why she had to take it; it was my confirmation from the Lord of Psalm 84:10.

A few weeks later, we had another lovely surprise. God had not finished confirming that we were in the right place. Another friend kept asking Ian what cut of steak is the nicest. Ian had no clue as to why she kept asking him, but once again, God knew. The Lord had impressed upon her heart to buy a card to go with the gift of meat and a bottled of mulled juice as a leaving present. It was her time to move on.

She had no idea of what was happening in our lives or our prayers even though I thought God had finished giving us confirmation. On the front of the card was a lighthouse standing on the edge of some rocks. She apologised for the card to which I replied, "Please don't. It is God giving us another confirmation." She was surprised as we told her the whole story and glad that she had been obedient and now understood.

We have an amazing God and Father, and He is always faithful.

The first time God spoke to me about being a gatekeeper at Pierrepont, was a few years ago on 23rd August 2012, but I had not understood what He meant, Now, all these years later, God has brought to pass what He had said back then. The rest of the year was spent relaxing and blessing people in our new home that God had given us for this next season. Now I was left wondering what He had in store for our next season and new year.

CHAPTER TWENTY-ONE | **Butterflies and Transformation**

I was shopping for a new diary with my daughter when one caught my eye. It had a picture of a butterfly and a bicycle on the front. Butterflies symbolise transformation and a bicycle is a mode of transport. I was not sure at the time what the Lord was showing me.

I found out later, when someone told me that a bicycle is not as fast as a car but it is quicker than walking. My verse for this year again is Isaiah 43:19 Behold! I do a new thing, now it shall spring forth, shall you not know it?

A second verse for this year and my life is, Psalm 19:14 Let the words of my mouth and the meditation of my heart be acceptable in Your sight, O Lord my strength and my Redeemer.

I am not saying this is always the case with me but when I say or do something that is not pleasing to Him, He is always gracious to forgive me, pick me up and get me back on track.

Our first assignment for the year was to upgrade some of the rooms, as they were looking tired and unloved. I had a plan to remove the coloured bed linen and to use only white bedding. NETS rooms had coloured linen and trainees washed their own bedding. I approached my manager and he approved it. The rooms were painted using a neutral fresh colour and the white linen looked lovely.

One of the women that came to do NETS1 told me of a dream that she had. In the dream, she walked into a beautiful room with white linen on the bed. I was so surprised and told her that God had shown her that in her dream as this was the first time NETS trainees had been given white linen.

How amazing is God to confirm once again to us that we are hearing His voice? I woke up this morning to the song, Great is Thy Faithfulness[8]. He is always faithful whether at work or in our private lives, even when we do not see it or feel it, He is always working, always faithful.

God has said to me on more than one occasion, "You cannot talk the talk unless you walk the walk." I believe that this will be a year of learning this lesson. It is to let your yes be yes and your no be no. We cannot walk and talk differently, what comes out of; our mouth must be in line with our heart and our walk otherwise we become like a clanging bell.

The Kingdom of God is also a Kingdom of words.

Proverbs 18:21 The power of life and death is in the tongue, and we give authority to whatever comes out of our mouth.

Romans 4:17 Call those things that are not as though they are…

Genesis 1:3 shows us the power of God's words as He spoke things into being and so do we.

Mark 11:23-24 Jesus is telling us to speak to the mountain, not about the mountain.

We all know these scriptures, but do we believe them?

Sometimes we tend to forget or, as my Pastor says, we leak!

It is so easy to forget and allow things to overcome us instead of us overcoming them. I am amazed at how quickly things can be turned around when we bring Jesus and the word of God into a situation. As

---

[8] Thomas O. Chisholm (1923) Great is The faithfulness Public Domain

we practice it more, the more natural it becomes; part of our speech. I remember somebody saying, do not look at how big the problem is, tell the problem how big your God is.!

As I am writing this, God is reminding me of my armour.

I remember when I was very young that we always dressed up for Saint David's Day at school. All the children would come dressed in traditional Welsh dress to commemorate St. David, the patron saint of Wales.

God reminded me about the story of David and Goliath that the armour the King had given David did not fit him as it was made for somebody else. (See 1 Samuel 17)

So too the Mantle God has for each one of us is made by God for His purpose. He makes it to fit perfectly and we have no need to wear other people's armour. It is not one-size-fits-all from our Lord.

God has a purpose for all His children. We are unique and so is our calling.

Mark 11:23 (Jesus speaking) For assuredly I say to you, whoever says to this mountain be removed and be cast into the sea and does not doubt in his heart but believes that those things he says will be done, he will have whatever he says.

Zechariah 4:7 Who are you, O great mountain, before Zerababel you shall become a plain

and He shall bring forth the capstone with shouts of 'Grace, Grace to it.'

This was a message of the day from the Lord as I read my daily devotion.

Amen and amen.

CHAPTER TWENTY-TWO | **A New Season**

The next six weeks will be a time of un-downing your nest, for many have grown accustomed to the place where your nest is, but I will be removing the down from your nest. This removal will propel you into the future that I have for you.

Do not be discouraged from the pricking you undergo over this next six weeks for this pricking, and the pricks you hear coming, are part of the un-nesting that will propel you higher as you begin to be pushed into the next dimension of your destiny. This is my time of pushing you forth. Mercy will come and come again. I have people rising to the fray of this land, shout 'Let there be light', declare this is the time of my calibration.

This time is to enter the preparation of the next level of ascending.

I was reading this devotion (I cannot remember who wrote it), and I felt God speak very loudly to my spirit that this was a new season in my life; one He had spoken about. I had a question come into my mind, What is the difference between being comfortable and being content?

The Lord gave me the answer. Being comfortable is a destination - being content is part of the journey.

My next thought was that God is preparing us to move! Wrong!

I spoke to a long-term friend and confident and shared with her what I believed God was saying and she reminded me that sometimes it is not a physical move but a spiritual move. As I thought about what she had said, I realised that she was probably right, and it seemed to make more sense as God had not told us to move to a new house yet, plus the fact that we had only just moved into the cottage a little while before.

We always want to know what God is doing but there are things that He does that we do not need to know; we just need to trust Him to do what He does best and be obedient when He asks us to do something.

One of my team members told me that this morning God had given her a picture of me. She said God sees me as a little girl kneeling down by my bedside and waiting on Him day and night, and also to tell me that I will not be disappointed.

Thank you, Lord, for this beautiful picture. As I sat with Him, this song came to mind, The Battle belongs to the Lord.[9]

Amen, that is something we really need to learn.

I used to find it very difficult to stay still in one place, sitting still for any length of time but as God had been teaching me to be still and know that He is God (Psalm 46:10), I have found it easier and easier to do.

Over the years, I have found that I am not the only one to find it hard. I often say to people to whom I am ministering, "What does your quiet time look like? How often do you sit with the Lord and say absolutely nothing?"

So, my question to you, reader, is the same one. How often do you sit with Him and just be?

I remember the first time that I sat with the Lord, He said, "I did not make you a human doing - I made you a human being!"

---

[9] The Maranatha Singers, The Battle Belongs to the Lord, Maranatha Music, 1989

To sit at His feet like Mary is an amazing privilege, just sitting and listening for His voice, just being with Him and not running around doing is so sweet.

I have learned that when we do this on a daily basis, we can receive everything we need for the day. Our daily bread, just as the people of Israel received their Manna daily, we, too, receive from God the things we need for the day whether it is physical or spiritual. I know for myself that He gives me strength to carry out my work as I rest in Him daily.

As I sat with the Lord this morning, I was suddenly aware of His presence, and I waited for Him to speak. I had been reading a book called, The Gatekeeper, and the Lord had been teaching me through it about being the gatekeeper of my mind. This is what came into my heart as He spoke: the gate is a spiritual position, being at the gate is an honour and a privilege.

I shared this with one of the leader's and he reminded me that it was also a place of judgement. The bible often mentions that the judges sat at the gate. I did not even think of it like that and certainly did not think myself a judge as there is only one true judge. However, I was humbled to hear the Lord say that being at the gate, living at the gate was an honour and privilege, it certainly is. I agree it is so, even though it is not always easy, but I am sure that it is worth it.

He is our treasure, and hopefully one day, we will hear, well done good and faithful servant. (Matthew 25:21)

We were watching a video called, Invisible[10], this morning at team time and I was left feeling just like the woman in the video. Sometimes I feel invisible.

---

[10] Invisible Directed by Pablo Giorgelli, Vitrine Filmes, Brazil, 2017

As I watched, I felt the Lord saying that He sees me. He reminded me about the dream of the water carrier that had been shared with me a while ago. He reminded me once again that I am His water carrier and even though the pots are cracked, He chooses to allow us to water the people that He presents for prayer. His rivers of living water flow out through the cracks and His light shines through us. What a privilege and honour to be one of His cracked pots.

2 Timothy 2:20-21 in a large house there are dishes and pots not only of gold and silver, but also of wood and clay. That is some are meant for honourable use and some for dishonourable use. If a person keeps himself free from defilement by the latter, he will be a vessel set aside for honourable use by the Master of the house and ready for every kind of work.

Today is the final day of my 40-day fast, and today being a Thanksgiving Day; we thank God for everything that He has done in us, through us and for us. For everything large and small, that He provides for us.

We know that You are God of the mountains and God of the valleys.

You will never leave us nor forsake us,

we trust You to get us to the other side.

God uses everything for His glory. We thank Him, as without Him, we can do nothing. As I sat with Him just reflecting on the year so far, and the years gone by, He took me back to March when He was un-downing the nest.

He showed me that this was a specific un-downing necessary to take me up a level.

He reminded me that I cannot talk the talk unless I walk the walk. I often find that I need to listen closely to what He is saying and then I repeat it back to Him in my heart just to make sure that I have heard right before I speak it out.

Paul says in Philippians 4:11 that he had learned to be content in whatever circumstance he found himself in, because he had learned the secret of being content. I believe the secret was to keep his eyes always looking up to God.

Psalm 121:1 I will lift my eyes to the hills from whence comes my help, my help comes from the Lord who made heaven and earth.

The more lessons we can learn from the Teacher, the more we can trust Him and know Him, one day at a time on our journey with Him.

God is a God of multiplication and if we truly trust Him, He can and will multiply us and take us deeper in Him and stretch our borders.

When we arrived at Pierrepont, Ian and I came with a suitcase each and we were given a lovely room with a shower en-suite. We were very grateful to God, as we did not know anything except that He had it all in hand. A few months later, we were offered a flat that had two rooms, a bedroom, bathroom and a lounge/diner and kitchen. To our surprise, a few years later, we were asked to move into the gatehouse, which is amazing.

We are grateful to God not just for the blessings, but for who He is. He is faithful and keeps His promises and His covenant with us. Why should we doubt Him? He is who He says He is and does what He says He will do. His timing is always perfect, but we need to trust Him and His timing, something we seem to find hard to do.

On occasion, we also try to help Him, but He does not need help. He does need us to trust and wait for His instruction. I have learned to do the things I know to do, and leave the rest to God.

This was the conversation with the Lord this morning and this is what I believe He said. "Stay calm, be patient. Your time is coming."

We know that His time is not the same as ours, but we need to trust that He has everything under control and if we will allow Him to lead, He will show us the right path to follow.

As we humble ourselves under His mighty hand, He will raise us up.

James 4:7-10 Humility cures worldliness, therefore submit to God, resist the devil and he will flee from you. Draw near to God and He will draw near to you, cleanse your hands, and purify your hearts. We do our part; He certainly does His and more.

Today my team and I are presenting Team-Time. How eagles get their young out of the nest to learn to fly is the subject.

I had found a short DVD on YouTube that we were able to watch, and the team had been given words of encouragement to share after watching it.

This came after the Lord had walked me through the un-downing six weeks ago, and now I understood why, although I did not at the time. He was preparing me to speak about the lesson that He had taught me in trusting Him.

Even eagles need a push sometimes and when a baby eagle does not want to leave the nest, the mommy literally pulls the nest apart so eventually there is nothing left on which her young can rely They have no option but to fly off.

The message is that God wants us all to be eagles. Proverbs 3:5 Trust in the Lord and lean not to your own understanding, in all your ways acknowledge Him, then He will level your paths.

A friend of mine used to have a picture of a bulldozer and the words; This is how He levels your paths.

Isaiah 40:31 but those who hope in Adonai will renew their strength, they will soar aloft as with eagle's wings, when they are running, they won't get weary, when they are walking they won't get tired.

He teaches us through faith and the question is Will you trust Me?

He wants us to fly like eagles and wants to teach us through the difficulties and the uncomfortable times to trust Him.

It is not an easy process, there is no formula, and He does it because He loves us, just as the mother eagle knows that her offspring would not survive just staying in the nest she has to make a hard decision and push her little one out. She is also teaching that little one to trust her because, as it falls, flapping about like a chicken, she swoops down and catches it. She then takes it back up to the partly broken-down nest and the whole process starts again. This goes on until the baby eagles has the confidence to fly. When it does, it is beautiful to behold.

Learn to wait on Him and He will raise you up, so again the question is- Will you trust Him?

Joshua 1:9 have I not commanded you? Be strong and of good courage, do not be afraid, nor be dismayed, for the Lord your God is with you wherever you go.

As I sat quietly with Him, not saying anything but just listening for His voice, this is the scripture that came to mind.

Isaiah 49:8 here is what Adonai says: 'At a time when I choose, I will answer you, on the day of salvation, I will help you, I have preserved you and I have appointed you to be the covenant for a people, to restore the land and to distribute again it is ruined inheritances to their owners.'

I do not know what this means or entails in the purpose that You have for me Lord, but I receive it and trust You that it is all in Your timing and in Your way.

I saw a picture of an olive tree; they can grow for 100 years or more. John 15:5 You are the true vine, we are the branches, we have been grafted into the vine, without You, we can do nothing.

I pray that we bear fruit that will last. Amen

We heard a teaching on the restoration of Peter, although it was slightly different. The Lord first tested Peter's faith and showed him what He could do by pulling him out of the water. Then in his brokenness, after he had denied Jesus, he was restored and baptised with fire by the Holy Spirit. He was then able to go and achieve what God had called him to do. He was no longer full of himself but was submitted to God and filled with the power of the Holy Spirit.

I believe this is the same for all of us. We, too, need to go through a process of being tested, humbled and then restored to Him for His use.

This afternoon, a friend came and gave me a word of encouragement: The power is coming. She gave me this word not knowing what God had been talking to me about. She continued to quote Jeremiah 29:11 I know the plans I have in mind for you, says Adonai plans for your well-being, not for bad things, so that you can have a hope and a future.

I realise that refining is not easy, but it is something we all must go through if we want to follow Jesus closely, so that we might shine for Him, and He will shine through us.

Today was not what I would call a good day except for the fact that God had made it. I was working through a situation with God that had occurred earlier. My way of dealing with things that come against me is to pray and work at the same time. The work takes away the frustration as I am talking to the Lord, forgiving, and blessing the person that hurt me. I was busy doing this and trying not to affect anyone else, as I just wanted to be alone and talk to God in my heart the same time.

While I was busy dusting and cleaning, a friend that works on reception, Elisha, said, "Sue there's a lion by the side of you." As I really was not in the mood to speak to anyone, I pretended that I had not heard her, so she came over to me and said again, "Sue there's a big lion by the side of you."

Immediately, as she said it a second time, I saw a mental picture of a lion standing upright. It reminded me of Aslan from the Chronicles of Narnia[11], she put her arm around my shoulder and said, "God says, He's got your back."

So much peace came upon me at that moment and suddenly I felt so much better. Later on, that day at around 4pm, Elisha and I crossed paths again coming in through the side entrance of the house; she looked at me and said, "Sue He is still there, He is still with you."

I could not see Him, but Elisha could, and I love it when God encourages us and knows when we need encouragement.

---

[11] Lewis, C. S., The Chronicles of Narnia. Harper Collins Publisher, 1980, USA

CHAPTER TWENTY-THREE | Yom Kippur

Today is Yom Kippur, the day of atonement.

Matthew 12:36-37 Moreover I tell you this, on the day of judgement people will have to account for every careless word they have spoken, for by your words you will be acquitted and by your words you will be condemned.

This is a very serious scripture, but I wonder how many of us take our words seriously. Me being one of them that have been taught by the Lord a while ago about what comes out of our mouths, but as I have said before and to others, we leak.

God is so gracious but if we insist on not watching our mouths, He will remind us, as He did this day.

This day was a day of prayer and I had built a habit of tacking Isaiah 55:11 onto the end of my prayers. So is my word that goes out from my mouth - it will not return to me unfulfilled; but it will accomplish what I intend, and cause to succeed what I sent it to do.

This day, as I did so, God spoke very loudly to my heart but I did not understand what that meant. To cut a long story short, I found myself arguing with God that I knew what the scripture meant. Wrong! Do not argue with Him, He is always right and continued to show me that I did not understand the scripture.

Suddenly I had a vision of a neon laser coming from my mouth; it opened to show me it was full of words. God then asked me, "How did I create the world?"

"Lord, You spoke it into being! You said, 'let there be light', and there was light!"

He then took me to Isaiah 57. We create the fruit of our lips

then to James 3:10-11 Out of the same mouth comes praises and curses, this should not be so.

I felt as though Jesus said; hot and cold water cannot come out of the same tap.

I got it. I had that revelation of my mouth; we give authority to whatever we speak and so we need to tame our tongues so that we do not use it to praise God and then curse people.

I remember God saying to me, "If you can't say anything good about somebody, then don't say anything at all."

I am learning this lesson daily and hope I am better than I was.

Paul says in Philippians 3:12 it is not that I have already attained or am perfected, but I press on that I may lay hold of that for which Christ Jesus has also laid hold of me.

I was taught by my Pastor to keep short accounts with God, so when I stumble, I repent and give it to God quickly and also ask Him to help me and cleanse me with His precious blood. I realise that we are all human and we are being sanctified daily. None of us are perfect this side of heaven, but it helps our walk with Him as we learn to trust Him more.

October seems to be a significant time of year for us, so as we took a week away. We went down to Wales to a beautiful retreat called Ffald-Y-Brenin.

I had been given their book called The Grace Outpouring, and God had been using this to train my tongue and teach me about speaking blessings over the country and families etc. as I started to do this He moved in my heart and did such a work in me that completely changed the way I speak and think.

God said, "We are blessed to be a blessing.' We accepted that mantle that He gave us, and He is faithful to stand behind His word to perform it.

As well as being a special time for Israel with the Feasts of the Lord, Sukkot, Tabernacles and the Jewish New Year, it seems to be a time of refreshing for Ian and myself. For the past few years, we have been led by the Lord to take a holiday and He lays on our hearts, where we should go.

I do not know what His purpose is for doing this, but we get to do something exciting together and rest and have a good time with each other. As I am writing this sentence, the Lord touched my heart as if to say, "This is the purpose: for you to enjoy timeout and be with each other outside of the work environment!" I was not expecting that.

CHAPTER TWENTY-FOUR | **Hiddenness and Manifestation**

I have just started reading a book called Hiddenness and Manifestation[12].

it is about stories of Divine Interventions. While reading, I was reminded of what I would now call, a Divine Intervention, although at the time I did not recognise it as so.

I worked for an interior decorator as the quality control supervisor, but we did not have a private toilet, so we used the public toilet, which was a minute away. The facilities were kept immaculate, as this was a tourist area and well known. As I walked in, I saw a woman with long grey hair drying it with a towel. It looked as if she had just washed it in the hand basin. I greeted her, "Good morning," as I was leaving.

As I reached the end of the corridor, I felt the Holy Spirit telling me to go back.' I fell into conversation with her and it felt as if I had known her all my life. This happened three times altogether as the Holy Spirit kept sending me back. Each time I spoke to her was better than the first. I felt so drawn to her, she was so full of love it was amazing. Eventually I asked if I could give her a hug, as she was so lovely, I really wanted to hug her. When I hugged her, I cannot begin to tell you what love I felt, it was like I was hugging my grandmother or even my own mum. It was so lovely I did not want to let go.

---

[12] Cooke, Graham, <u>Hiddenness and Manifestation</u>, Brilliant Book House, 2003, USA

I do not know if you have ever had an encounter like that, but I could not explain it. I asked her where she was from and she told me, "From all over." She was very small in stature and even shorter than me, and I am only 4ft 10ins. She looked very frail and was pulling one of those shopping trolleys behind her. As we carried on chatting, I asked her if she knew the Lord and she said, "Oh yes! And He told me to say thank you for taking time out of your busy day to speak to me."

When she said it, her face lit up like the sun with such a big smile. I said good bye to her, and we parted our ways. As I walked back to the workshop, I had a scripture come to mind, sometimes we entertain angels, and we don't even know it. (1 Hebrews 13:2)

There was something so special about this woman and I have never forgotten that encounter. I arrived back to the workshop and thought I would like to bless her with some money to buy lunch, but I could not find her anywhere.

I often think of that God appointment and still am reminded that we are hidden but not forgotten. God hides us for a purpose and when the time is right, He will unhide us and reveal to us His purpose.

I sometimes wonder if I will ever meet her again, even in heaven.

I had been battling with thoughts of being forgotten and so I asked the Lord what was going on. I was surprised to receive a message of affirmation from a friend. "God wants you to know how important you are and what a crucial job you are doing as the gatekeeper at Ellel. He also wants you to know that you are exactly where He wants you to be and that He is proud of Ian and you."

I am always humbled when God does this, especially when you are not expecting it. On this the last day of October and the holiday, this is the word that came to mind this morning, The darkness cannot overtake the light, who is Jesus. He also reminded me about the Dragonfly and transformation.

I include it here as it spoke to me and I am sure that it will speak to the heart of whoever reads this book.

The devotion is called Standing in Big Shoes.[13]

Joshua 1:5 No man shall be able to stand before you all the days of your life, as I was with Moses, so I will be with you.

Imagine how Joshua must have felt when God told him that he was to take the place of Moses and lead the Israelites into the promised land. Moses was an amazing leader, who would want to try to fill his shoes?

God told Joshua that he would succeed not because of anything that he had done in the natural but because God was with him.

Moses was successful because God was with Him, God told Joshua the same thing would hold true if he believed.

God kept encouraging Joshua to be strong and confident, to take courage and not to be afraid. In other words, He told him to believe. Put your faith and trust in God, He will give you the strength to stand and accomplish whatever He asks you to do. Believe me when I say that I am speaking to myself also as I am writing this, it encourages my heart to know that God is not a respecter of persons, He does not have favourites and what He did for them, He will do for us as we walk with Him and trust Him.

I am reminded of this as I am reminded by the Holy Spirit that I need to write this book. As I did not believe that, I had it in me to write a book, I have procrastinated but eventually repented and asked God

---

[13] Standing in big shoes (The story of Joshua after Moses had died) You Version Bible plan

for help. As I have been writing, the Holy Spirit has given me words to include that I did not think about, but it surely makes sense.

It has been a privilege to walk with Him and to be taught by the MASTER.

I want to say Thank You, Lord, for Your patience and Your faithfulness, knowing that You will never leave me nor forsake me.

As I close the doors on another year, I believe God works all things together for those that love Him and are called according to His purpose. (Romans 8:28)

CHAPTER TWENTY-FIVE | A Year of Progress and Acceleration

This year, I believe is to be a year of progress and acceleration. Sometimes we can feel that nothing is happening and one-year just melts into the next. Christmas comes and goes, then the New Year comes and goes, and nothing seems to change. We are still in the same place, doing the same thing day in and day out. We do the mundane things, but as we do, God is busy doing something in us that we do not see.

We all have stories to tell, and this book is just a small part of my story.

God writes the story of our lives, and our stories are ongoing as we walk with Him. The stories in this book are over a period of ten years and it has been a privilege to walk with Him. The deeper we go with Him, the more we see ourselves as we really are and sometimes it is not a pretty picture. We need to be true to ourselves and allow God to cleanse us and sanctify us.

it is not easy but it is worth it as I'm sure everyone's prayer is that we become more like Jesus. Jesus teaches in Luke 14:25-34 about counting the cost. This is something we need also to be aware of. We need to count the cost before we try to start building. He also says that whoever does not bear his cross cannot be His disciple.

In between all the mountain top experiences, there will also be the valley experiences. I believe it would not be true to only write about the mountain tops without at referring to the valleys. The mountain tops are great but it is in the valleys that we grow. In the valleys, we learn to trust and know God better and know Him as our Father who will never leave us nor forsake us.

He is the God of the mountains and the God of the valleys.

When I fasted at the beginning of the year, my devotions were about the water level rising.

Ezekiel 47:3 With a line in his hand the man went out toward the east and measured a thousand cubits [one-third of a mile] and had me wade across the stream; the water came up to my ankles

I felt the water level rising and by the time I reached day 21 of my fast, so much had happened. God kept encouraging me through His word and by sending people across my path with an encouraging word for me. The start of this year was the hardest one I have experienced in a long time.

As I sat one morning contemplating this year so far, this came to mind.

I am a child of God,
I am chosen,
I am holy,
I am set apart,
I am a royal priest,
I am righteous,
I am because He is,
He has blessed me and clothed me in Himself,

I am a daughter of the Most High God because of His Son the Lord Jesus Christ who rescued me from darkness and brought me into His glorious light.

Then the song Cornerstone[14] came flooding into my whole mind and being, that my life is built on nothing less than Jesus Blood and Righteousness.

Thank you, Lord, that You are always with us through the storm. You never fail to get us to the other side. You are in the boat with us. A friend of mine once said his father always called God, the Captain of the ship. He certainly is, if we let Him. Going deeper is challenging but He is with us all the way.

I dreamt that I was playing a card game with my husband and somebody else, but I could not see their face. The game is called, DON. It is a game Ian taught me some years ago. I was extremely excited, as I had a really good hand, a full house, everything I needed to win. Needless to say, I was smiling from ear to ear, as I knew I would win the round. It was the last day of my fast and I felt that the Lord was showing me that winning was symbolic of winning with Him.

As mentioned, the beginning of this year was not easy, but God helped me through it and has taken me into the deeper water with Him. My prayer is that He takes me in so deep that I cannot put my feet on the bottom; I have to swim.

I attended a prayer meeting with all the prayer ministers and as I was leaving, Charity, an intercessor, was instructed by the Lord to anoint my right ear lobe, right thumb and right big toe.

Charity said that God has anointed my ear to hear His voice, my thumb for His work and my toe to walk where He wants me to go.

Psalm 91:2 I will say of the Lord, He is my refuge, my fortress, my God in whom I trust. Thank you Lord for Your mercy and grace.

---

[14] Hillsong, Cornerstone, Hillsong Music Publishing, 2011

Zephaniah 3:17 The Lord your God in the midst of thee is Mighty, He will save, He will rejoice over you with joy, you will rest in His love, He will joy over you with singing.

I have developed a habit of writing a daily letter to God, although in saying this, sometimes I forget if I am busy at work. I do spend time with Him but then I forget to write it down, so I find that I am writing down for a couple of days. I used to do, what we call journaling, and then one day, as I was in the library, I was drawn to a DVD called, Letters to God[15]. It was a story about a young boy that wrote a letter to God every day as a prayer. I just thought it was so much more personal than journaling.

I started to write letters to God instead of journaling. I write my thoughts then what I believe God is saying to me. Also, instead of using a normal exercise book, I bought a new diary at the beginning of the year so that I could keep a timeline of the entries. (Funny I did not think of it like that until I started writing) When you think of it, it makes sense. While we are walking with God, we have an accurate time of when He said whatever it was He said. I am always amazed when I look back at my letters of how much God has done through the year and all the things I have prayed, and also all the answers He has given.

As I have said previously, sometimes we leak. I have found there are times when I have had a word from the Lord and I remember it clearly, and then there are other times that I forget. I think that these are the times that Jesus was talking about when He was teaching about the seed falling on rocky ground; the enemy steals the word from us. We need to remember God is outside time and He can take

---

[15] <u>Letters to God</u>, Directed by David Nixon, Cinedigm Entertainment Group, United States, 2010

us back to that place and remind us of the Promises that He has given us. He can also minister to us in those areas that still have authority and heal us.

These are a few things that He has said to me over this period that I actually forgot about and as I am writing this book, He is also reminding me.

We shall not be afraid of evil tidings because our hearts are fixed trusting in the Lord.

Proverbs 13:22 The wealth of the wicked is laid up for the righteous.

Money has a mission and it is crying out to be in the hands of the righteous, and when He gives us wealth, it is to establish God's covenant on earth.

1 Corinthians 15:58. Therefore my beloved be ye steadfast, unmovable always abounding in the work of the Lord, for as much as you know that your labour is not in vain in the Lord.

1 Corinthians 13:4-5 Love is patient and kind, not jealous, not boastful, not proud, rude or selfish, not easily angered.

Psalm 27:14 Wait on the Lord, be of good courage and He shall strengthen your heart, wait I say on the Lord.

This is a picture the Lord gave me, and I thank You for it, Lord, it reminds me of the Lion of Judah and that I am safe in Him, and He protects me.

Father, my prayer is for anyone reading this is that they open their hearts and receive from You. I thank You that You always hear us when we speak to You, even when it is just whisper, if I can hear You when You whisper then I know that You can hear me when I whisper. I remember being in the Holy of Holies with You and it was so quiet that I was whispering to You as I did not want to break the quiet with my voice.

Child of God, He hears all your whispers, all your cries for help, He knows your heart and everything that you have been through, He knows your fears and catches your tears. Open your heart to the Father today and give everything to Him, He says to cast all your cares upon Him as He cares for you.

Sometimes, I walk down to the river and break bread with the Lord and drink from the cup, but I also keep back a bit of bread and throw it in the river, symbolically casting all my worries and cares upon Him.

Often we do not even realise that we are worrying, trying to stand in our own strength. Been there - done that!

Psalm 16:8 (NKJV) I have set the Lord always before me, because He is at my right hand, I shall not be moved. Whoever shall confess that Jesus is the Son of God, God dwelleth in him and he in God.

I listened to a speaker this morning about butterflies and the spiritual significance of a butterfly (transformation)

There are times when we are growing into butterflies, but we do not see how beautiful we are. We tend to focus on the other side of us, but God does not see that once we have been born again. Just like the caterpillar evolves in the cocoon, so we as children of God grow into a butterfly as God does His work in and through us.

So, let's take a step back here and listen to what God is saying! What is God saying to you right now?

How do you see yourself? Do you see a butterfly?

We do not realise how beautiful we are, when Nicky said this, I realised that I too think the same way about myself, but God touched my heart and I felt Him say, "You are beautiful in My sight" This is true for you too.

As you just sit for a moment, see yourself as a butterfly. What colour are you? Do you have large, beautiful wings, or are you of the petite variety? Whichever way, you are beautiful in His sight.

Maybe draw a picture of yourself as a butterfly on a blank page. Ask God to show you, He will! You are beautiful in His sight!

John 11:25 Yeshua said, ' I AM the resurrection and the life, whoever puts his trust in Me will live, even if he dies and everyone living and trusting in Me will never die.

Do you believe this?

John 7:38 He that believes on Me as the scripture has said, 'out of his belly shall flow rivers of living water.' God showed me a while ago that it won't be a trickle but a river like Niagara Falls. Amen

Donne was woken up at 1.00am one morning by God to write this poem for me.

I dedicate this to her and in remembrance of her soft gentle nature. This is what she wrote down. God says this to you.

He delights in all His flowers in His garden,
your beauty caresses Him and He takes pleasure from your radiant bloom.
He says that you are resilient, strong and upright,
you grow even under the harshest conditions.
He says you are like a Barberton Daisy,
you do not wilt under the blazing sun, or extreme drought.
The rose He says is delicate and sweet,

but you continue to give pleasure long after the rose petals have drooped,
died and fallen to the ground.

The Lord says He sees you like this:

Picture in your mind a desert, dry, parched, hot, the sun beating down from a deep blue sky, nothing stirring except the wind. However, right there in the midst of the barrenness, a single flower, a sudden burst of life. He knows your blossom is deep and crimson in colour and your stem is firm, resilient and green because you drink from His fountain.

He knows your circumstances are hard and difficult at the moment, but He sees you standing there, your petals beautiful, your eyes fixed on Him. standing firm and bold in the desert, blooming and radiant against all odds and giving much delight and joy to those close enough to smell your sweet aroma.

RESILIENT ● BOLD ● STRONG ● UPRIGHT ● BEAUTIFUL ● SWEET AROMA.

Allow God to speak to you through these words today.

This was ten years ago but as I said previously, God is outside time and so He brought this back to my remembrance so that I could relate to what He is saying to me now. A Barberton daisy grows best in dry arid ground, but as soon as it gets a few drops of water it has a beautiful orange bloom, and it opens wide to show how beautiful it is.

Recently, the marketing team acquired a new camera lens and wanted to try it out, A few of us were asked if we would have our eyes photographed.

Imagine my surprise when I saw the picture of my eyes, the inner part next to the pupil was orange and looked just like an orange daisy.

As I stood in the kitchen this morning, God spoke to my heart, "You have amazing eyes. They are the windows to my soul." The bible says in Matthew 6:22 The lamp of the body is the eye, if your eyes are good, your whole body will be full of light.

Matthew 5:14 You are the light of the world, a town built on a hill cannot be hidden.

As we walk with the Lord, we walk humbly with a contrite heart. We might make mistakes, but You are always teaching us, training us, and You get us through the hard times. We would rather walk on the narrow road with You than walk on the wide road that leads to destruction.

Lord Jesus, help us to grow in every circumstance and give us strength to endure, for we wrestle not against flesh and blood but against principalities, powers and rulers of this dark world. (Ephesians 6:12)

Help us to understand the heavenly protocol to wrestle against spiritual wickedness in high places. Making sure that we cover all the bases and understand Your ways and Your heavenly courts, taking away the authority of the enemy. Just as in a legal battle, the rights of the offender are taken away so that justice can prevail.

Thank You that You are patient to teach us these principals and You lead us and guide us until we learn and understand.

Matthew 6:33 seek first the Kingdom of God and His Righteousness and all those things will be added unto you, for where your heart is your treasure is there also.

I am reminded of this, and my question to you is the same: Where is your treasure?

This book is part of what God has done in my life, but there is so much more that I have not included. There's an old song that is normally sung at Christmas time.

Lord, You are more precious than silver,
Lord You are more costly than gold.
Lord You are more beautiful than diamonds,
And nothing I desire compares with You.[16]

Can we, sing this to Him and totally mean every word, at any time, not just at Christmastime.

---

[16] DeShazo, Lynn, Lord You are more Precious than Silver, Integrity's Hosanna! Music, 1982

CHAPTER TWENTY-SIX | Praying for Open Doors

I have recently been praying for God to open doors. I realise that it is God that opens the doors that no man can close and also that we need to wait on God until He opens them. When I look at King David and all the giants of the bible, they waited on God all the time before they made a move or decision. If it is good enough for them, then it should be good enough for us.

The problem is we live in a culture of fast this and fast that. We live in a world where we need it yesterday. It is quite hard when we know God has said something but we do not see anything happening. That's when our faith grows and becomes stronger. I do not think it gets easier, but we do have more peace and the word of God says to let the Shalom which comes from the Messiah be your heart's decision-maker, for this is why you were called to be part of a single body. (Colossians 3:15)

When we do not hear His voice, then we check if we have peace in our heart.

A friend once gave us a word that God would be opening doors for us in Wales and that he saw us going through the doors. I prayed and gave it to the Lord. If it were from God, He would bring it to pass. I had peace but then he said something that I did not have peace about, so I quickly renounced anything not from God and spoke blessings over him.

We need to test every word given to us and give it to God for judgement. The bible tells us to be vigilant and to test everything, as false prophets will say things that is not from God. Test the word as it should resonate as confirmation to what God has said, and also look at the fruit in the person's life.

I have included this to remind us that we need to test words given; even if they are from friends, we should have peace in our hearts.

Galatians 6:22 Bear one another's burdens; in this way you will be fulfilling the Torah's true meaning which the Messiah upholds.

Thank you, Lord, that You waste nothing but work it all for our good and for Your glory, and when the fog clears we will see what You have done and see it clearly.

As we worshipped this morning, this word came to mind: In every revival, God raises up a prophet.

I have been praying for revival for a while, and as I read my devotional, I learned about the prophet's job. The job of the prophet is not to direct the revival or to lead it but to interpret it. Brokenness and confession are what the prophet discovers and what the participants in revival experience. I did not understand why God had shown this to me so, again, I gave it back to the Lord and trust He will show us in due time.

A song came to mind as I was praying for revival in our land.

Thank You for the cross Lord,
Thank You for the price You paid.
Thank You that the cross and what You did is the anchor for my soul.

I believe You were born of a virgin,
I believe You are the Son of the Most High God,
I believe You gave Your life on a cross willingly to save us,
I believe You died and rose again,

You are now seated at the right hand of the Father,
and we are seated there with You in Christ Jesus,
I believe that all authority to was given to You in heaven
and on earth and under the earth and the gates of hell cannot prevail.

You have given us Your disciples the authority to tread on snakes and scorpions and all the power of the enemy, for greater is He that lives in me than he that is in the world.

Send revival Lord to this land once again and make this a land that fears the Lord.

Amen

CHAPTER TWENTY-SEVEN | When God Gives a New Name

A while ago, God put a date in my heart; it was 17/7/17. I asked the Lord, "What is so special about this date?" I kept asking but did not seem to get an answer, so, I gave it to Him and asked Him to hold it until the right time. I believe sometimes if God told us immediately, then we would try to make things happen ourselves and it would end up in the flesh.

I remembered the scripture in Luke when Jesus was missing. Mary and Joseph found Him but did not understand the statement, which He spoke to them saying, did you not know that I must be about my Father's business? However, Mary kept all these things in her heart. She also had to wait and see what God was doing. So, just as I did not have an answer about the date 17/7/17, I also had to wait.

I kept it in my heart and waited for the day to come. As the year went on, I had forgotten about it, although I did write it down. The Lord taught me to write things down whether it is a vision as in Habakkuk 2:2 Write down the vision and make it plain on tablets, that he may run who reads it, for the vision is for an appointed time, but at the end it speaks, and it will not lie. Though it tarries, wait for it, because it will surely come, it will not tarry, or when He gives us a word.

When we write it down, we have a record of what God has said, then we can go back and re-read the words He has given. God establishes His word concerning us.

Isaiah 46:9-11 Remember the former things of old. For I Am God, and there is no other; I am God, and there is none like Me, declaring the end from the beginning and from ancient times, things that are not yet done, saying, ' My counsel shall stand, and I will do My pleasure. Calling a bird of prey from the east, the man who executes My counsel, from a far country.

Indeed, I have spoken it; I will bring it to pass, I have purposed it; I will also do it

.Reading my bible this morning, I was drawn to read outside of my reading plan. Suddenly I was reminded about 17/7/17, as the date was 17/7/17. I started to read Genesis 17:7 and realised that this chapter is when God changed Abram's name to Abraham and also Sarai's name to Sarah. As I read these verses, I felt that God was changing my name from Susan to Susannah. Also, that He was saying, "My covenant is with you and your descendants after you in their generations, and is an everlasting covenant to be God to you and your generations after you."

I also did some research on why God sometimes changes people's names. I found out that it is because He wants to show them a new mission or assignment in life and to assure them that His divine plan would be fulfilled in them.

I received this but did not do anything about it. I did speak to Ian, but it did not go any further. This scripture came to mind, that God is not slow in keeping His promises as some people think of slowness, on the contrary, He is patient with you for it is not His purpose that anyone should be destroyed but that everyone should turn from his sins. (2 Peter 3:9)

Hebrews 9:11 (NKJV) Also, that Christ came as High Priest of the good things to come, with the greater tabernacle not made with hands, that is, not of this creation, nor with the blood of goats and calves but with His own blood He entered the Most High Place once for all having obtained redemption.

I had a picture of the Ark of the Covenant. Thank You, Lord, that You took Your own blood and offered it as a sacrifice for the world.

I recently watched a movie called, The Shack.[17] Having read the book a few years ago, I was curious to see their interpretation. The movie came to the part where the main character went to meet WISDOM. Part of the scene was that he had to sacrifice one of his children, as he wanted to be judge. He then said, "No! He suddenly realises what Jesus had done for us. He had not done anything wrong but had given His life in our place.'

Through the tears, I imagined Him doing that for us and our children and families. He did it even while we were still sinners.

Let us pray for our unsaved families, that they would come to Him, allow the Holy Spirit to speak to your heart right here and now, ask Him to touch your heart and give you words to pray for them.

Peter asked Jesus, how can they be saved, and Jesus answered, what is impossible for man is possible with God. Praise God. (Matthew 19:26)

Luke 18:27 (Jesus referring to salvation) it is He who touches hearts to reach out together.

Amen... Thank You, Lord, that it is YOUR WORK.

When God does something new in our lives, it can sometimes feel quite scary, especially when we do not know where we are going or how we will get there. However, God is always faithful and will get us

---

[17] The Shack, Directed by Stuart Hazeldene, Lionsgate Summit Entertainment, 2017

to where He wants us to be, at the right time in the right place as we follow Him and do the things He is asking us to do. We are learning to listen for His voice and be obedient.

Ephesians 3:20 Now to Him who by His power working in us is able to do far beyond anything we can ask or imagine, to Him be the glory in the Messianic community and in the Messiah Yeshua from generation to generation forever. Amen.

Joshua 1:9 Have I not commanded you, be strong and of good courage, do not be afraid nor dismayed for the Lord your God is with you wherever you go.

God sometimes reminds me that as He was with Moses, so is He with me. (Joshua 1:5) He was with Joshua and all the people that He has called to Himself, wherever we go and wherever He sends us. He goes before us and prepares the way for us, He opens doors that no man can close, He protects us and defends us because we are His children, and we trust in Him and do not lean on our own understanding. (Proverbs 3:5) As we seek His face and His plan for our lives, we can do the things that He has called us to do.

As Joshua made an ongoing choice to repent of sin and focus on the Lord to lead, guide and direct then we follow his example.

We seek God's face and His will and plan in humility and obedience to His instruction, fearing God and valuing God's opinion over man's opinion so that the promises He gives us will come to pass in our lives.

When our hearts are open and willing, He is able to do anything in us and through us. For everything, there is a season, a right time for every intention under heaven. God's timing is always perfect and as we wait on Him, we ask Him to help us not to run ahead or to lag behind, we wait and listen for instruction from heaven.

Galatians 6:9 So let us not grow weary of doing what is good, for if we don't give up we will in due time reap the harvest.

At the beginning of the year, somebody asked me if I was expecting a hard year. I replied that I did not, but whatever happens I know that God is with me and He will get me through. I do not know about you, but when someone comes out with a question like that, it can be a bit of a shock, or you could start worrying or thinking about what could happen.

In these times, we need to focus on the Lord and not let those words come to rest in our hearts. It has turned out to be a year of difficulties, but He is in the boat with us and as we trust Him and call on His name, He answers us and gets us to the other side. Life happens but we keep our eyes on Him.

My Pastor says it is just a moment in time, and I suppose that when we compare it to eternity then that is all it is - A MOMENT.

Hebrews 12:1-2 So since we are surrounded by such a cloud of witnesses, let us too, put aside every impediment, that is the sin which so easily hampers our forward movement and keep running with endurance in the contest set before us, looking to the author and completer of that trusting Yeshua, who in exchange for obtaining the joy set before Him, endured execution on a stake as a criminal, scorning the shame and has sat down at the right hand of the Throne of God.

This scripture reminds me that we do not do this alone, we have the Father, Son and Holy Spirit on our side, and we are being cheered on in the heavenlies by the cloud of witnesses to keep on keeping on, because without faith it is impossible to please God. (See Hebrews 1)

More about the name change later on.

The Lord reminded me this morning of Niagara Falls and how it flows so freely over the ravine. He also reminded me that small streams become rivers and sometimes they can be as wide as Niagara Falls. I believe the deeper we go with Him and in Him, we become like Niagara Falls and Living water flows through us to others just like that. There's a song we used to sing with the line, There's a river flowing over me (I forget the rest). We used to sing it way back when I did not even know the meaning of the words as I was not born again but how amazing is God that He brings these things back to mind to show us that even when we did not know Him, He was still working in our lives.

I had read the biography of Katherine Kuhlmann and towards the end of the book she said, "Lord, I want to be your water carrier." I said the same thing, "Lord, I want to be Your water carrier in all seasons, lead me and guide me by Your Holy Spirit. You are the Living Water that flows from the Throne, and I draw from You to give to others." Amen.

One day, as I was praying for a woman, I was with another prayer minister and the Lord gave her a picture of water pouring from my hands into hers as I asked the Lord to fill her up with fresh living water. She saw water flowing from my hands into hers and cleansing her blood and going into her veins by the Holy Spirit.

How awesome that He sometimes shows us what He is doing. Thank You, Father God, Lord Jesus and Holy Spirit.

CHAPTER TWENTY-EIGHT | The Battle is The Lord's

As the end of the year draws near and we push to finish on a high with Him, it is amazing how He speaks to us. For me it is very often a song that will spring up in my heart, I have learned that this is one of the ways He speaks to me. I have also learned that this is also one way that we fight our battles. When Joshua went out to battle at Jericho, God instructed him to put the musicians ahead of the priests with seven trumpets. (See Joshua 6) I believe that when we sing praise to God in a situation, then darkness has to flee as light, and darkness cannot be in the same place at the same time.

I remember one time when I was not in a good place, I had a tiff with my husband and a friend said to me, "Go to the garden and praise and worship God." I had only been there for a few minutes, but I felt the release of anger and hurt as God came into the situation and the enemy had to flee. Amen.

I love the song by Michael W. Smith, This is how I fight my battles.[18]

As I woke up one morning, I woke up with this song:

"Don't worry about a thing, cause every little thing is gonna be alright".[19]

---

[18] Michel W. Smith, Surrounded (Fight my Battles) written by Elyssa Smith, UPPERROOM 2017

[19] Bob Marley, Three Little Birds, Universal Music Corp, 1977

It was so loud that I started to laugh, God has an amazing sense of humour.

This verse came to mind, Isaiah 41:13 For I Adonai your God say to you as I hold your right hand, have no fear I will help you.' And the eyes of Adonai watch over us who wait for His grace to rescue them from death and keep them alive in famine. He is our shield, and our hearts rejoice because we trust in His Holy Name. May Your mercy be over us Adonai because we put our hope in You.

Just as King David, Joshua and all the other greats of the bible asked God what we shall do next, Lord, how do you want us to do this? then how much more should we be asking Him.

How much more should we ask the Holy Spirit to lead and guide us, He knows the plan and we need to be asking Him to show us. In the Old Testament, the Holy Spirit would come upon certain people to do God's will but now we have the Holy Spirit living in our hearts. How awesome is that. As I have walked with the Lord, I have learned to rest in Him and sit with Him daily. The Holy Spirit is my best friend, as I know that I can tell Him anything and He does not go and speak to other people about any problems I may be facing, but He helps me see them in a different light, He helps me to see them from another perspective. There is always two sides to a story, yours and the other person's, or yours and God's. when we decide to see things from another perspective, God is able to change our heart and take out the rocks and stones and to make more room for His Holy Spirit.

There's a song that I just heard recently called, Make Room (in your Heart) by Casting Crowns, which is an amazing Christmas song, I had never heard it before yet the words so touched me I was singing it without even realising it.

We need to make room in our heart for the Holy Spirit, as He needs us to give all of our heart to Him so that He can use us for His glory. The words of the song say, so that God can write His story in us for His glory[20]. Amen to that.

The Lord promises that when we go through water, we will not drown, they will not overwhelm us, and also when we go through the fire, that we will not be scorched, the flame will not burn us. As I was reading, I remember the Lord speaking and saying to my heart, "Learn as much as you can and leave the rest to the Holy Spirit."

I believe that God spoke to my heart and called me to be a prophet, but He said, "You are to be a different kind of prophet."

I remember the first time He said that I did not receive it, as I was so afraid of what it might entail. I had a very hard childhood, and my father was not the easiest person to relate to, but he loved us in his own way. He would punish us, sometimes harshly, but he would not allow anyone else to touch us, which sometimes got him into trouble.

I must be honest here that sometimes I felt like Jeremiah and told God so. I always seemed to be crying and weeping about something. I believe now that it was God doing a healing work in me, and now that I know better, I am happy to be called of God, to be used by Him how ever He wants.

Romans 5:3-5 But not only that, let us boast in our troubles, because we know that trouble produces endurance, endurance produces character, and character produces hope, and this hope does not let us down because God's love for us has already been poured out in our heart through the Holy Spirit who has been given to us. Our hope can only be in Him and in His plan for our lives.

---

[20] Make Room, John Mark Hall, Matt Maher, Lyrics © ESSENTIAL MUSIC PUBLISHING, Capitol CMG Publishing

Jeremiah 29:11-12 For I know what plans I have in mind for you, says Adonai, ' plans for well-being, not for bad things; so that you can have hope and a future. When you call to Me and pray to Me, I will listen to you. When you seek Me, you will find Me, provided you seek for Me wholeheartedly; and I will let you find Me,' says Adonai.

God spoke these words to His people Israel when they were in exile, but He wanted them to know that He still loved them and had plans for their lives. He says the same things to us, when we mess up and the enemy tries to tell us that we have gone too far this time, when we turn back to God and are seriously repentant, He is always faithful and just to forgive our sins and cleanse us from all unrighteousness.

1 John1:9 He has us in the palm of His hands, and He will never let us go.

As I read my devotional this morning, this stood out. The things that irritate you are the things you are designed to change, but I also realise that by seeing it from a different perspective and by allowing us to be put in the other persons place, it gives us new vision to our eyes to see with His eyes.

Our wedding anniversary is a week before Christmas, so we had a day out at the coast. We often go to Portsmouth for a day out just to watch the ships and ferries coming in, there is just something about watching water that we love.

We were walking through the town and spotted a homeless person and felt that the Lord wanted us to speak to him. As he shared with us how he had become homeless, a sense of compassion filled our hearts and again it was as if God was allowing us to put ourselves in his position. We shared what God had laid on our heart and blessed him, we left him in a better place, and he said that he actually felt the presence of God as we spoke to him. It was a privilege to pray for him.

Father, would You bless him and water that seed that was planted by Your Holy Spirit, that it might bring a harvest into his life that would glorify You.

Father, I thank You for all that You have done through this year and as we start a new year, I am excited to see what You will do, so, once again, as I fast, I thank You that You keep me strong.

CHAPTER TWENTY-NINE | Times and Seasons

The word I received for this year is a Time of Fulfilment. I believe God will cause us to achieve His purpose for this year. A year to cross to the other side, the uncommon side and that He will allow us into our Goshen - our broad place. I expect God to do this. He has a plan for our lives and He will prepare us for whatever He will be teaching us throughout the year.

God has laid on my heart that He wants to train me for the Deborah anointing, I do not know what it entails but I trust that He will do what needs to be done, and so once again, I humble myself under His Mighty Hand.

This year, I am called to be a woman of wisdom and discernment, not to run ahead but also not to lag behind. Sometimes I find myself running to keep up with God. My prayer is Lord, help me to understand the seasons of the call. As God's call is still unfolding in our lives, it is wise to stop, listen and reflect on what we have learned so that we might understand the season; to understand the cycles, patterns and times that He has designed for implementation in our lives.

Help us, Lord, to grasp Your purpose for our lives and understand time correctly.

I was led to study the book of Deborah for this time and also to meet with my mentor as I fast and pray. Deborah was a judge in Israel and was raised up after all the rulers had ceased. God brought people around her to help her.

She was also a prophetess and a wife; she was the wife of Lapidot and she sat under Deborah's palm between Ramah and Biet-El in the hills of Ephraim where the people of Israel would come to her for judgement. God also used her to instruct men in the battle for the Lord. She was a worshipper and gave all the Glory to God. (See Judges 5)

Deborah was anointed with power and designed for influence because God could trust her to do the right thing with what He had given her.

She did not abuse the authority that He had given her but used it to glorify His Name. I remember my Pastor always said, it is not about who is right, but what is right. We should always have integrity, meaning we are the same when we are being watched or when we are not being watched.

For me, the first week of a fast is sometimes quite challenging as God pulls the weeds up and starts preparing the garden of my heart for new seed. He has always referred to my heart as a garden and as I read the scripture of the different soils, it makes sense that He should use that analogy.

When Jesus was teaching, the parable He told was of a farmer who went out to sow his seeds and the different soils those seeds encountered. (Matthew 13:1-23)

As He speaks about the different soils, He makes it clear that the rich soil is the one that bears the best fruit. In addition, if we think about the preparation that a farmer has to do beforehand, it makes sense that God would need to prepare our hearts before He can plant new seed. When we understand what Jesus is teaching, He is teaching about our hearts.

When God is doing something new in our lives, the enemy will always try to sabotage us, but we have Jesus to help us.

Matthew 6:33 Seek first the Kingdom of God and His righteousness, and all these things will be added unto you.

Proverbs 16:3 If you entrust all you do to Adonai; your plans will achieve success.

It is very important to ask God for confirmation. We need to be alert because the enemy will try to deceive us. Not everything that looks like God, sounds like God or feels like God, is God. Gideon asked God three times for confirmation, just to make sure that he was doing the right thing and that it was God speaking to him.

I am reminded that when we are on the cross, we cannot look behind. We can only look forward and ahead with God. The enemy always tries to keep us looking at our past but we need only look at what Christ has done on the cross and what He said - it is finished. Jesus did everything for us and now it is up to us to appropriate it, as in our walk with Him, knowing our authority in Him. When we have confessed our sins to God and asked for forgiveness, we are forgiven, we need to receive this by faith and not look back again. When it is under the Blood, do not go fishing in the Blood.

1 John 1:9 If we confess our sins, He is faithful and just to forgive us our sins and to cleanse us from all unrighteousness.

We need to take God at His word; if He says it is done, then it is done.

Hebrews 12:2 Looking to Jesus, the author and finisher of our faith, who for the joy set before Him endured the cross, despising the same and has sat down at the right hand of the Throne of God.

God will always honour what we give to Him from an attitude of gratitude and even more so. There's a song that I love singing to the

Lord called Simple Token by Vineyard. The song starts with, all I have to offer is my heart laid bare.

One day, I was in a really bad place and I started singing it to the Lord. Suddenly He stopped me in mid-sentence and said, "That is all I want, I just want your heart."

The Lord gave me another word that day: You will always have enough to go wherever you want to go.

We have always had more than enough to go and do what we wanted and also to give out of our abundance to somebody that is in need. On more than one occasion when we needed to take a break, God has blessed us with the necessary finances. We always managed to get the best deals for holidays etc.

I always find it amazing that things happen quickly when we pray and give it to God on open palms.

As I reached the end of my fast period from the beginning of the year, a friend from South Africa sent me a message to say that He had given me, new wine and a fresh new anointing. It is always a privilege to have confirmation from somebody that does not know what is going on or what God has been doing. I believe that is a true confirmation. God's confirmation.

I am reminded of Zechariah 4:11-14 where it speaks about the olive trees and especially the receptacles of the two golden pipes from which the oil drips.

As I was reading my devotional, these are the words that touched my heart deeply. Empty yourself so He can fill up the oil, the two golden spouts filled by the Holy Spirit.

I thank You, Father, that when I ask for wisdom, You give me wisdom.

Thank You for this new year, new wine and fresh oil; thank You for the planting of the new seed and watering it by Your Holy Spirit that the harvest will come to glorify You. Amen.

Romans 8:28 Furthermore we know that God causes everything to work together for the good of those who love God and are called in accordance with His purpose.

As I write this book from my journals, I am reminded of all the things God has done in me, through me and for me, and today is no exception. I am reminded that as we commit our way to ADONAI and trust Him – He will act. (Psalm 37:5)

Joshua 1:9 Haven't I ordered you, be strong, be bold don't be afraid or down hearted because Adonai your God is with you, wherever you go.

Today God gave a colleague a picture of His hand upon me as an encouragement. We all need encouragement even when we think we do not, but He knows exactly when we do.

Romans 8:39 Neither powers above, nor powers below, nor any other created thing will be able to separate us from the love of God, which comes to us through the Messiah Yeshua our Lord.

Have you ever had a thought in your mind that you cannot seem to shake off? Recently I have had a thought that we would be moving to a new house. We have been here at Ellel Pierrepont for eight years in August, but I cannot seem to stop thinking that we will be moving. A few years ago, I had asked the Lord when we would be moving. He replied that when the time comes, I would know. As I reflected on my year, I had a strong sense that we would be moving back to Wales, which is something I had sensed since we came back from South Africa. More about that later.

We do not have finances to buy a new house but we know that God does and He has always been faithful to provide for all our needs. What would be different this time? if He is calling us to move to Wales, then He will supply all our needs according to His riches in glory by Christ Jesus. (Philippians 4:19)

Ian had been trying to persuade me to go back to South Africa for a holiday but as we had lived there so long, it was more exciting for me to visit places that we had not seen. For some reason, this year was different, and suddenly I had a desire to go back and visit friends and revisit our church. We decided to save all our leave days and all our money so we could have a three- week holiday, which would also include a visit to Dubai to spend time with Paula, our daughter. This year we asked the Lord if we could travel to Dubai and then to South Africa and also to help us be wise with the best route. Ian found out that we could get a round trip with an airline that would enable us to have ten stops if we needed.

It was amazing that by the end of February, we had booked and paid for the whole three-week vacation. During the rest of the year, God was at work giving us peace.

As I sat with Him this morning, I saw a picture of a door where there should have been a window. As I looked to see what God was saying, I noticed the colours of blue, red and green. I know that blue = royalty and authority in the spiritual realm, red = the Blood of Christ and green signifies that He takes us into green pasture with quiet waters. For some reason I could not make out what He was trying to show me, but as I shared this with a friend, suddenly he said, "God will make a way where there seems to be no way."

God gave him the interpretation of the picture and it made sense immediately. God was showing me that He makes ways when there seem to be none. The window became a door that He was opening for us to take a break.

This morning I was prompted to share about thanking God for our unsaved families. Instead of just saying they were not saved, we should add the word, yet! When we add the word yet, at the end of it brings hope to us that they will come to know the King of Kings and Lord of Lords. It is a powerful statement of faith and our words are powerful but sometimes we do not recognise it. We need to be alert to what comes out of our mouth.

Isaiah 55:11 so is My word that goes out of my mouth – it will not return to Me unfulfilled but will accomplish what I intend it to do.

Our words are powerful whether we speak negatively or positively. Either we give God authority or the enemy. Sometimes we can start speaking blessings but when we do not see change, we stop. It does not happen overnight but when we persevere, it will happen. The secret is to keep trusting God and keep speaking His word. My Pastor used to call it, working the word.

I have been writing from my journals and I have been reminded of things that God has said and done. I had forgotten so much and now, five years later, I am seeing many things happen although some have already happened.

I believe the Lord wants us to persevere as we come to know Him better and our relationship with Him grows.

1 Timothy 6:12 says to fight the good fight of faith, take hold of the eternal life to which you were called when you testified so well to your faith before many witnesses.

While we at communion this morning, we received a word from the Lord about our calling and one word struck a chord within my heart: God has not changed His mind about you.

Moreover, for you, dear reader, I would say the same. I do not know where you are or with what you are struggling, but I do know that God has not changed His mind about you. When God calls us, He does not change His mind and say sorry I made a mistake.

Romans 11:29 for God's gifts and calling are irrevocable.

He is the same yesterday, today and forever and He does not make mistakes. He will also give us confirmation of our calling as He tests and trains us.

Isaiah 48:17 Thus says Adonai your Redeemer, the Holy One of Israel.

I AM the Lord your God who teaches you for your own good, who guides you on the path you should take.' For all scripture is God breathed, and is valuable for teaching the truth, convicting of sin. Correcting faults and training in right living, thus anyone belonging to God may be fully equipped for every good work.

Do you ever have those days where nothing seems to go right? Well today seems to be one of those days but I have learned that when God is busy with us, especially when He gives revelation, the enemy will come and try to steal that which the Lord has spoken. He comes to steal the Word from our hearts. It is one of those times that we need to be strong in the Lord and the power of His might. It is one of those times when we stand and hold our ground and use scripture as Jesus did.

Revelation 12:11 and they overcome by the blood of the Lamb and the word of our testimony.

I guess when we feel like that, it is so easy to want to give up but that is not an option for us. The only way to go is forward, find somebody that is trustworthy to pray with us and help us to stand.

2 Corinthians 4:16 This is why we do not lose courage, though our outer self is heading for decay, our inner self is being renewed daily.

2 Corinthians 5:14-16 for Christ's love compels us because we are convinced that One died for all and therefore all died, and He died for all that those who live should no longer live for themselves but for Him who died for them and was raised again, so from now on we regard no one from a worldly point of view.

God sorted out my heart once again, and took me deeper in Him. I must admit, it is not easy when God is at work in us but it is worth it. He loves us so much and is continually changing us into the likeness of His son, Jesus Christ.

I was reminded this morning that God's word to us comes as seed to be planted in our hearts and the heart needs to be prepared just as soil in the ground, some 30, 60- or 100-fold harvest. Amen. Then God's Shalom, surpassing all understanding, will keep your hearts and minds safe in union with the Messiah Yeshua.

CHAPTER THIRTY | **All Change**

Every year I take on a new team of young people to be trained to work in the housekeeping department. Some of these youngsters have never had to clean rooms or toilets but they learn quickly and have hearts of gold. They are so eager to learn and help. It can be hard for them especially if they have not been away from home before, but God is gracious as He teaches them new skills.

They come from all over the world to be discipled and to take a year out for the Lord. Some even put off college or university for a year if they believe it is God's direction for them. What is amazing is this; He not only teaches them but teaches me too.

One young man said to me, "Sue, remember when you ask God for patience, He does not just dump it on you, He gives you a situation so that you can use your patience." Needless to say, God has a sense of humour too.

Thank you, Lord, for all these young people that you bring. They are a blessing and a joy to work with and it is a privilege to be part of their lives and for them to be part of mine.

Proverbs 17:17 A friend shows his friendship at all times, it is for adversity that such a brother or sister is born.

These young people grow such a great friendship together and also with us as leaders. This morning I received an encouragement from a friend in South Africa. She is a long-time friend and even though we are back in the UK, we still chat on a regular basis. God seems to know exactly when we need to be encouraged, I had gone through quite a few battles of late, so I needed a bit of encouragement.

Maybe you are in that place too that you need a word of encouragement. As you read these words, know that the Lord your God is with you, He will never leave you nor forsake you and He will get you through whatever the situation. Jesus is in the boat. A friend in South Africa said that his dad always said, Jesus is in the boat, He is the Captain. Is He the Captain of your boat? If He is not, then ask Him to be the Captain of your boat right now. He is always willing to oblige.

The word of encouragement was as follows:

I look at you and I am proud of you. After so many battles and challenges that you have faced, some lost and others defeated, you have triumphed. I believe you are a great warrior, a housekeeper, a peace maker. You are standing there with great faith, you are adorable, and no-one will bring you down because God is the One that sustains you, my warrior friend.

Thank You, Lord, for all Your words of encouragement for me and for whoever is reading this at the moment. Pour out Your fresh living water onto Your children and refresh them with Your Holy Spirit. Let their lives reflect Jesus in them as a love offering to You. Be glorified in their lives, Lord God.

I am always very grateful to God for all the words of encouragement that He gives me for others. We do not know what people are struggling with so when you give a word of encouragement to them and they tell you what has been happening, it is amazing.

So how does God encourage you? Do you recognise it when He does or do you dismiss it as just a thought? As He sends people across our path, it will usually be someone that you trust or knows you better than most. Sometimes God even brings a song to mind. I have learned to listen to the words as He speaks to me through the song.

As I was watching a movie, God reminded me once again of the power our words hold. We can both break and destroy or we can build up.

Proverbs 18:21 The tongue has power over life and death, those who indulge in it must eat its fruit.

When you think deeply about this verse and recognise what God is saying, it can be a revelation and what we speak will change.

Psalm 23:1-3 The Lord is my Shepherd, I shall not want, He makes me to lie down in green pastures, He leads me beside still waters, He restores my soul, He leads me in the paths of righteousness for His Name's sake.

Thank the Lord that when we are in the valleys of life we can sit with Him and enjoy His company. Sitting at His feet is the most amazing place to be.

Pray with me as you read:

You are my Shepherd, and You lead me and guide me.
Thank You, Lord, that in Your presence I am changed,
I have heard Your voice and felt Your touch deep in my heart,
I love You Father God, Lord Jesus and Holy Spirit,
So, as I come to You and enter Your gates with thanksgiving and Your courts with praise,
I bless Your Holy Name and open the doors of my heart to You,
for who can ascend the hill of the Lord, only those with clean hands and a pure heart.
So, cleanse my heart, Lord, from anything that is displeasing to You,

for You are my refuge and my fortress, my God in whom I will trust.

Amen.

My devotional this morning said:

Lord open our hearts to the joy and wonder, the sobriety and the fear of the covenant relationship with You, lead us O King out of the superficial and into the supernatural, lead us into a covenant with You for our families and our Nation. Amen.

Matthew 7:7 Keep asking and it will be given to you, keep seeking and you will find, keep knocking and the door will be open to you.

2 Thessalonians 3:3 ...but the Lord is worthy, He will make you firm and guard you from the evil one.

We humble ourselves under the mighty HAND OF GOD and He will raise us up.

Philippians 3:13-14 Brothers for my part I do not think of myself as having gotten hold of it, but one thing I do, forgetting what is behind me and straining forward toward what lies ahead, I keep pursuing the goal in order to win the prize offered by God's upward calling in the Messiah Yeshua.

As we walk with the Lord and learn to hear His voice and how He speaks we get closer to Him.

I remember watching a movie about superheroes. I do not often watch movies of that nature, but it was on, so I decided to watch it. In one scene, the hero had been thrown out of his home and was speaking to his brother up in the galaxy somewhere, and his brother heard him.

Suddenly God intervened and I heard Him say very clearly to my spirit, "That is how I hear you when you speak to me, but I am closer."

Even if we whisper, God hears us, and even if we only speak to Him in our heart, He hears us. This brings me to a testimony that I was watching on You Tube. A very lovely young woman who had suffered with an eating disorder for many years was testifying that Jesus is real and that He had saved her; she is now a born-again believer and follows Him.

She said, "I did not pray or say it out loud that I was calling for help, in my mind I just said, 'JESUS' and an amazing love flooded over me which I will never forget, who else could love me like that?" She gave her life to Christ a little while later.

Maybe as you read this you are battling with some kind of affliction, maybe it has touched your heart too, maybe you know the Lord but not as intimately as you would like. So, as you sit with him now in a quiet place, just whisper His name, JESUS and allow Him to love you, to hold you as a child.

Lord when I gave my life to You, I saw You standing in front of me, You stepped forward and wrapped Your arms around me and later You gave me a picture of Yourself on a white horse; You rescued me just like a princess and a knight. You revealed Yourself to me in an awesome way. I understand Lord that it is not the same for everyone, but You are my REDEEMER, and You came to my rescue. I am so glad that You did.

Psalm 16:11 You make me know the path of life, in Your presence is unbounded joy, in

Your Right-Hand eternal delight.

I am realising more and more that God only withholds things until we are able to receive that which He has for us. I suppose if He did release everything at once, not only would we get a bit prideful but we probably could not hold onto it. Sometimes we can be overwhelmed when He shows us something new and that is the time to ask Him to help us grow more. It took me a long time to understand from Him that He had called me to be a prophet. I immediately thought of Jeremiah being put into the water tank and all the other things that he had done to him. It honestly frightened me=; I was not ready to die quite yet!

I finally received it after three times of being called and even though I have received it, I still think about this verse.

1 Samuel 16:7 but Adonai said to Samuel, ' don't pay attention to how he looks or how tall he is, because I have rejected him. Adonai doesn't see the way humans see- humans look at the outward appearance but Adonai looks at the heart.

I do not know how God will use me, but I do know this. He has cleansed my mouth and uses it. He is training me and developing me in His time for His glory and in His way, all I need to do is be obedient.

Whatever God has called you for, it is for His glory and He will give you everything you need to do His work. The gifts and callings of God are irrevocable. This is what I believe He has been doing this year. Your efforts are not in vain, God sees everything that you do even when others do not. He is honing you to be an arrow in His quiver and when you are ready, He will pull you out for a specific purpose and then put you back and hide you until the next time. Remember God has not forgotten about you, so do not let the enemy tell you lies, you are in the quiver to rest until He gives you another assignment.

1 Corinthians 15:58 so my dear brothers, stand firm and immovable always doing the Lord's work as vigorously as you can, knowing that united with the Lord, your efforts are not in vain.

Hebrews 12:1 So then since we are surrounded by such a cloud of witnesses, let us too put aside every impediment that is sin, which hampers our forward movement and keep running with endurance in the contest set before us.

Romans 12:12 That we rejoice in hope, be patient in your troubles and continue steadfastly in prayer.

Therefore, as we digest His word let me speak a blessing over you. I love the Aaronic Blessing in Numbers 6:24-26:

May the Lord bless you and keep you, may He make His face to shine upon You, may His countenance be upon you and may He give you peace, Amen and Amen.

Psalm 34:8-9 The Angel of Adonai who encamps around those who fear Him, delivers them. Taste and see that Adonai is good, how blessed are those who take refuge in Him.

Psalm 18:30 With You I can run through a whole troop of men, with my God I can leap a wall.

This morning I was reminded of a word given to me back in 2016:

Make your flesh ready as the blessings that I am going to pour out will be so much that you won't cope if you do not prepare yourself - PREPARE.

I was standing in reception today when a friend suddenly said to me, "I can see God's Hand upon you, Sue. I see His glory on you." What a privilege it was to hear that statement.

I prayed for a young man who had just suffered a terrible motorbike accident. He was the nephew of a colleague. I felt the Lord say to ask Him to heal his brain, so we prayed and asked God to reduce the swelling and heal his brain. This was my devotion verse that morning,

Psalm 116:1-2 I love that Adonai heard my voice when I prayed because He turned His ear to me, I will call on Him as long as I live.

I thanked God for His direction and for the words from His heart for this situation. A few days later, I heard that the young man had in fact been healed and that he was now out of danger and well on his way to recovery. I do not know if he knows the Lord yet, but his family was so grateful that God had answered the prayers.

Thank You, Lord, that You are still in the business of working miracles, and that You met him at his point of need even when in a coma.

1 Peter 1:3 Praise be to God, Father of our Lord Yeshua the Messiah who in keeping with His great mercy has caused us through the resurrection of the Messiah from the dead, to be born again to a living hope.

I am in awe of You Lord God, watching You at work and knowing that You hear us is a privilege and honour.

Talking about miracles, it was a miracle that my mind had been changed to go back to South Africa for a holiday. As I said earlier, Ian had wanted to go back for a while and I think he had been secretly praying and asking God to help. I think he was surprised when I agreed and one morning said to him, "Maybe we should take all our leave and have a good three weeks away and stop off at Dubai to visit Paula, and then fly on to South Africa for the other two weeks. He was over the moon. We made a travel plan and put everything in the order of travel.

We spent a lovely week in Dubai and then flew down to SA. Unfortunately, by the time we arrived in Whiteriver where we used to live, it was really late. The roads had changed so much that we could not find the Lodge where we were to spend the weekend. We decided the next best thing would be to stay in a Holiday Inn, but we could not find that either. It was gone midnight when we pulled into a petrol station to try to get some directions. We were both tired and very lost. As we pulled into the petrol station, suddenly two women came out of the shop, so Ian asked them about hotels or B&B's. We explained our story, and we were so surprised at how helpful they were to two strangers. They went out of their way to help us even to the point of taking us to the Hotel so that we would arrive safely. Well, I believe in angels and God had answered our prayer for someone to help us, big time. We thanked them and blessed them as they were like two angels sent by God to help us.

We had a beautiful holiday; catching up with old friends and church friends and even stayed with a couple that we have known for more than twenty years. We had visits to the Kruger Park once again and were rested, ready for the rest of the year. We arrived back in the UK refreshed and privileged to have prayed with some of the friends that we had left eight 8 years ago.

We held our annual Christmas Dinner with some friends; we thanked God for them and also prayed for them. It was a good year and was great to share a meal with people that support us and to fellowship with them as we celebrated the birth of our Lord. It is such a privilege to cook for them and to gather around the table with them. It is a tradition that we started in SA with our teams. it is to say thank you to them for their hard work through the year and I believe it is better than buying gifts that they may never use.

Jesus enjoyed fellowship regularly around the table, and there are numerous references to food in the bible; it is a blessing and gift to share one's food with others.

God has said that we are blessed to be a blessing and so we share our blessings with others.

Luke 6:38 Give, and you will receive gifts—the fullest measure, shaken together and overflowing will be put right into your lap, for with the measure with which you measure out will be measured back to you.

Not that we give to receive but it is a spiritual law. We are generous because He is generous to us. Blessed to be a blessing. We always thank the Lord for the provision that we can be a blessing to others in word, thought and deed.

I John 3:1 See what the Father has lavished on us in letting us be called God's children! For this is what we are.

The reason the world does not know us is that it has not known Him.

Isaiah 25:1 Adonai, You are my God, I exalt You, I praise Your Name for You have accomplished marvels, fulfilled ancient plans, faithfully and truly.

Thank You, Lord, that as seed is planted and watered, You will bring it to fruition and harvest to glorify You.

Today is our wedding anniversary and Adonai gave me a scripture: Habakkuk 2:2 Write down the vision.

God has taught me to write down all the words and pictures that He has given me over the years. I was reminded that these words etc. though they may tarry, they will come to pass, just as the word of God says. (Habakkuk 2:3)

In my office, I have a picture of a cottage that I drew randomly but do not know why. My vision is that it would be our home in Wales; a little larger than we have presently, with a conservatory and two decent-sized bedrooms in case our daughter comes to visit, situated on the edge of a village, in a quiet but not isolated area. Somebody has the keys and will bless us with the cottage for as long as we need it. I believe that God will open doors for us to minister to His people and also to speak about having a relationship with Him.

Psalm 46:10 Be still and know that I am God.

God put the desires in our hearts to come into agreement with Him so that He can give us the desires of our hearts.

He has blessed us so much and we are so very grateful, but again it did not happen over-night, we just kept being and doing what He asked us to do.

He blessed us with another trip to Germany to visit Ian's brother and his family for Christmas. it is a privilege to spend time with them.

We pray for them daily and I believe that they will meet Him one day, although one of them already is a believer.

Isaiah 9:6 In order to extend the dominion and perpetuation the peace of the Throne and Kingdom of David, to secure it and sustain it through justice and righteousness henceforth forever. The zeal of Adonai-Tzavot will accomplish this.

Once again, thank You, Father, for another year of walking with You, learning to trust You and Your ways, through the good times and the not so good times. You, Lord, are always with us and as we abide in You, You abide in us and You get us to where You want us to be.

Thank You for the touch of Your Hand upon our lives, THE MASTER'S TOUCH.

John 15 You are the real vine, and the Father is the gardener, You cut off every branch that does not bear fruit, You prune so that it may bear more fruit.

Amen.

This is Your Year

My prayer for this year is that I walk into the things that You have called me to do, that I will know who I am in You but also that I will know who You are in me even more than I do now. Without You, Lord, I can do absolutely nothing, but I can do all things through Christ who strengthens me.

As I watched a blessing by John Paul Jackson[21] (deceased), it touched my heart so deeply it was as if the Lord Himself was speaking to me through him.

My father had never spoken a blessing over me, and I received this from the Lord by faith. Can I encourage you as you read this right now to do the same, if you have not or did not ever receive a blessing from your earthly father or did not receive affirmation and encouragement, please receive this from me as a blessing over your life to encourage and affirm. Let it touch your heart as it touched mine, deeply, sincerely and may it reach your heart personally.

You can also find this blessing on YouTube, called The Blessing by John Paul Jackson.

I pray that you reach the purpose for which you were created,
may you have courage above your peers,
may you have more passion for the things of God than others think is possible,
may you choose wisely without earthly bias.

You have people to influence that you have not yet met, you have lives to change that are waiting for your arrival,

you are being strategically placed wherever God takes you by His grand design so you can become everything He has made you to be.

---

[21] The Blessing by Paul Jackson, www.youtube.com/@dreamsand_mysteries

That is a place where you can grow best, and a place where you can be most fruitful and a place where the future is changed because of your presence.

May you see vistas that others do not know exist and may you see God in every petal of every flower and every blade of grass for each of them are designed by His Hand.

May you bless your children that they would become giants in the faith under the Mighty Hand of God, you won't fail you were made by God for such a time as this.

Amen and amen.

Thank You, Lord, that it is not by might nor by power but by Your Spirit that this will be accomplished.(Zechariah 4:6)

Proverbs 16:9 A person may plan his path, but Adonai directs his steps.

As I fast and seek Your face, Lord, I thank You and give this year to You to lead and guide. You are the Captain of our ship Lord so take us this year into the place that You have for us.

As I read Daniel 10 this morning, it was as if the Lord was saying, "Do not be afraid - since the first day that you determined to understand and to humble yourself before your God, your words have been heard."

Every time I read this passage of scripture, it seems as if God is directly speaking to me, to reassure me that He had heard my prayers and even though I may not see anything happening, I know in my heart that He is busy.

When I fast at the beginning of every year, I believe that God receives it as my first fruits of my life for the year.

He is always gracious to do in me and through me the things He has planned for the year. As I have said previously, this is my walk with Him, and He says that I cannot talk the talk unless I walk the walk.

Maybe you can relate to what you are reading, so this could be a confirmation of what God is doing in your life. All I know is that He is always faithful, and He will lead and guide you as you walk with Him one day at a time.

Psalm 90:12 So teach us to count our days so that we will become wise.

If you entrust all we do to Adonai, your plans will achieve success, (Proverbs 16:3) and when we seek Him wholeheartedly, we will find Him.(Jeremiah 29:13) As we come close to God, He will come close to us (James 4:8), as we clean our hands and purify our hearts and not be double minded but, ' JUST BELIEVE.' He will make Himself known to us. As we meet with Him in that special place, He will meet with us and when we determine to make more room in our hearts for Him, He will make Himself known to us in ways that we could never think or imagine.

Read these scriptures at your leisure and ask God to speak to you personally.

Psalm 119:105
Matthew 5:6
Jeremiah 17:7
Psalm 103:5
Romans 10:17
Matthew 11:15
Matthew 16:24

One of the ploys of the enemy is to break up Christian marriages and he has certainly tried with Ian and me on more than one occasion.

However, God is greater than the enemy, and if we are willing to humble ourselves and allow God to do in us and through us things that need to be done, then He will restore back to us what the enemy has tried so hard to destroy. We all go through some fire with situations coming against us but the one thing we can do is stick together and allow God to be the third person in our marriage. He will put that three-string cord around us and help us to be united in the way that He ordained for us.

Lord I thank You for my family, husband, children, grand-children and great grand- children. Thank You that Your Hand is upon their lives and I speak blessing over them. Bless them and keep them, make Your Face to shine upon them, that Your countenance be upon them and give them Your peace.

As I watched a programme about Israel, it explained about numbers and that every year on the Hebrew calendar has a number. This year is 5779, which pertains to fruit bearing and expectancy of unusual faith.

Hebrews 11 speaks of men and women of faith that God used mightily but there are a few leaders not mentioned, although God used them all mightily.

Deuteronomy 8:18 says that we shall remember the Lord your God, for it is Him who gives you power to get wealth, that He may establish His covenant which He swore to your father as it is this day.

This is the covenant made with Abraham. We now have a new covenant through the Lord Jesus Christ with which He made with His own precious Blood, even better than the one He made with Abraham. All we need to do is receive it and believe it.

As I come to the last day of my fast, I am ready to receive the things that God has for me this year.

How about you? God wants you have the fullness of everything that He has planned for you, even before you were born. Won't you speak to your Father in Heaven and receive from Him the things that He is so eager to give to you?

As I watched a gardening programme, I was interested that the presenter was saying that he prunes the vines down because he is not interested in the quantity of grapes but the quality of the grapes. Suddenly I had that revelation of what he was saying, that this what our Heavenly Father does with us. He prunes us because He wants to increase the quality of our relationship with Him, to draw us closer to Him, to know Him more.

My prayer, Lord, is that we are enabled to bear fruit, fruit that will last and that we will bear fruit in season and out of season.

John 15:16 ... that it is You that chose us, and Your intent is that we bear fruit that will last.

And that fruitfulness will be our hallmark.

CHAPTER THIRTY-ONE | A Year of Knocking on Doors

Isaiah 22:22 The key of, the house of David, I will lay on His shoulder, so shall open and no-one will shut, and will shut and no-one will open.

I believe this year will be a year of knocking on doors to see which doors will be opened and which have been closed.

I had recently prayed for a child that had been diagnosed with autism. As you can imagine, the grandparents were understandably anxious, but we prayed together for this little one. Once we had prayed, we were excited to see what God would do as His presence was so tangible. Later on, I had the thought of checking the meaning of his name, Josiah, which means Jehovah, has healed. I believe that as we prayed, God was saying that he (Josiah) would be a miracle in progress.

As the weeks went by, I continued to receive good reports of how God was working in this child's life and how much more responsive he had become and how he was improving daily. God is amazing and does what He says He will do. All Glory to the Father, Son and Holy Spirit. Josiah is improving every day and his healing is ongoing.

Isaiah 55:10-13 For just as the rain and snow fall from the sky and do not return there but water the earth, causing it to bud and produce, giving seed to the sower and bread to the eater, so My word that goes out of My mouth, it will not return to Me unfulfilled, but will accomplish what I intend and cause to succeed what I sent it to do. Amen.

As we come to the mountains they will burst out into song and all the trees in the countryside will clap their hands, cypresses will grow in place of thorns, myrtles will grow instead of briars, this will bring fame to Adonai as an eternal imperishable sign.

Galatians 5:14 For the whole of the Torah is summed up in this one sentence, ' love your neighbour as you love yourself.

When we pray for others from our hearts, out of love, God responds, and we see miracles take place.

I attended the day of national prayer for the UK with a friend. We arrived early and the presence of God was tangible even before the day started. God was present, waiting for His children to pray for the nation.

Later in the day, people were being called to the platform to stand in the gap for their particular country, so I went up with a few others to represent Wales. It was an honour but also very scary to stand before the Lord God Almighty and ask for revival in the land. Solomon had been praying and God had responded saying to him that if My people, who bear My name, will humble themselves, pray, seek My Face and turn from their wicked ways, I will hear from heaven, forgive their sin and heal their land. (2 Chronicles 7:14)

As we stood on the platform, we all stood in the gap, confessed, repented and prayed and asked God to heal our land. The anointing was so strong that I fell on my bum and needed help to stand back to my feet.

Father, as we listen, learn and follow Your lead, help us not to have confident in ourselves but always to be confident in You. Thank You for the glimpses of Your Glory that You give us to become dependable servants for You.

My pastor would say that people do not want to know how much you know, but how much you care. The word of God says in 1 Corinthians 13:1, I may speak in tongues of men, even angels but if I lack love, I have become merely blaring brass or a cymbal clanging. As we stay united with Him, the vine, then we will put forth fruit, because without Him we can do absolutely nothing.

So, as we are raised along with the Messiah, and seek things above where He is sitting at the right hand of God, so are we there with Him. As we keep our eyes on Jesus, King of Kings and Lord of Lords, we will have peace knowing that He is in control, and whatever the situation the outcome will be for our good.

Psalm 34:9 says this: Taste and see that the Lord is good, how blessed are those who take refuge in Him.

When I first met the Lord, I had a picture of a bowl of fruit and ice-cream, and this verse came to mind. When I saw the picture, I did not understand what He was saying but now I know that the Lord is good to those who love Him and are called according to His purpose. The picture was to get my attention, and it certainly did.

The first time the Power of God came upon me, I was left weeping and trembling. I wondered what was happening but I suddenly realised it was the Power of the Holy Spirit. I was not afraid and I knew that He wanted me to be obedient.

I had to remove some objects from our home and when I had finished the task, I had total peace. Philippians 1:6 … and I am sure of this that the One who began a good work among you will keep it growing until it is completed on the Day of the Messiah Yeshua.

I wrote this letter to God as a dedication to Him and to thank Him for all He has done. I find it very peaceful to write a letter to Him and offer it up as a prayer and He is gracious to accept it. I am very aware of who He is THE GREAT I AM.

Lord You are the Great I AM, Creator of Heaven and Earth and yet You call us sons and daughters, those who love You and are called by Your Name.

I thank You that You never change but as we allow You to change us, we become more like Your Son Yeshua and You are glorified in our lives.

It is always a privilege to see You at work through us and to be vessels for You. We have nothing to offer anyone of ourselves and cannot give what we do not have inside. So, we humble ourselves under Your Mighty Hand and allow the Holy Spirit to do what only He can do in us and through us and the Glory goes to You.

Psalm 100:4-5 Enter His gates with thanksgiving and enter His courts with praise. Give thanks to Him and bless His Holy Name. For Adonai is good, His grace continues forever and His faithfulness for all generations.

Once again, my thoughts are about being led forth and guided by the Shepherd to where He wants us to be.

Thank You Lord that You are doing a new thing, and You are making roads in the desert, rivers in the wasteland. New thoughts about moving to Wales and to test that this is from God and not just my vain imagination.

Psalm 143:10 Teach me to do Your will because You are my God, and let Your good Spirit guide me on ground that is level.

As I pray for my family often, I am always grateful to God that He hears my prayers and also makes a way where there seems to be no way. Recently as I prayed for my daughter who lives in Dubai, the Lord answered a prayer for her for accommodation. It was affordable , in a safe and clean area and accessible for her work. It was a reasonable price and came with many extras. How good is our God, He knows all our needs and we are so grateful to Him for all that He does, sometimes it does not happen in the way we think but it happens when we need it. He is the same yesterday, today and He is still in the business of miracles, whether they are big or small, they are all the same to Him and nothing is too big for Him to handle.

Habakkuk 3:17-18 For even if the fig tree doesn't blossom and no fruit is on the vines, even if the olive tree fails to produce and the fields yield no food at all, even if the sheep vanish from the sheep pen and there are no cows in the stall, still I will rejoice in Adonai, I will take joy in the God of my salvation. It is good to worship and praise the Lord as we wait, for we know that He is faithful.

We had been praying for a friend's husband to return to the UK from Ghana for about eighteen months. He had to return to apply for a new visa and the time was growing shorter and shorter. He had to leave as the visa laws had changed and despite all the prayers, nothing seemed to be happening. We kept praying and worshipping God knowing that He had a time and a plan for them to be reunited. Then suddenly we received the really good news that his visa had been granted, we danced, praised and worshipped God, our true God and friend. We thanked Him for His goodness and His faithfulness and rejoiced together with them both. It was one of the best days ever and we all celebrated.

Hebrews 11:6 ...and without trusting it is impossible to be well pleasing to God because whoever approaches Him must trust that He does exist and that He becomes a Rewarder to those who seek Him out.

Jeremiah 33:3 Call out to Me, and I will answer you—I will tell you great things, hidden things of which you are unaware.

2 Peter 3:9 The Lord is not slow in keeping His promise as some people think of slowness, on the contrary, He is patient with you for it is not His purpose that anyone be destroyed but that everyone should turn from his sin.

God's timing is always perfect, never early, never late but sometimes we can over think what we hear or try to work it out in our own mind and get disappointed when it does not work out the way we are thinking, and we can allow ourselves to be deceived. God is gracious and when we ask Him, He will show us where we went wrong. Also, as we listen to counsel from others we then recognise that what we thought was God, actually was not. This can happen when we are tired and also when we want things to happen in our own time, or when we are not prepared to wait.

Today so many of God's family are waiting for answers for the next move forward While the pillar of cloud and the pillar of fire are busy moving slowly but surely, thus says the Lord:

Stand in the ways and see and ask for the old paths, where the good way is and walk in it, then you will find rest for your souls. (Jeremiah 6:16)

How awesome is our God who, when being the driver of our earthly vehicle, gives us peace knowing He is on the throne of our hearts, directing our steps.

Psalm 37:24 Adonai directs a person's steps, and He delights in his way; he may stumble but he won't fall headlong for Adonai holds him by the hand.

While we wait for the Lord to speak to us, His word comes into operation.

Isaiah 30:21 Your ears will hear a word behind you saying, ' this is the way, way walk in it, whenever you turn to the right hand or whenever you turn to the left,' yes indeed He will be our guide even unto the end.

I cannot say that I have not made the mistake of thinking I had heard from God yet questioning myself if I really had. I believe this is how we learn. I often ask Him to give me at least two or three confirmations so that I am sure. Not because I do not trust God but because I do not trust myself sometimes that I have heard correctly. I'm sure He does not mind and would rather we ask Him another time to be sure.

Earlier this year as I was doing the rounds of locking up, I met a couple of people in one of the rooms. As we chatted, I was told that God had given the one woman a picture of a Dahlia flower and it was for me. I thanked her but did not know what it meant or why God had given her the picture.

A whole year later, as I was reading my notes and listening for God's voice, I was prompted to look up the meaning of the name Dahlia. Some refer to it as a valley flower, and there have been many valleys this year, but this flower is also known to represent one who stands strong in his or her values.

The name in Arabic stems from the word for tip of the branch, especially that of a grapevine or an olive tree.

As the year progressed, multiple events have taken place such as our church closing and everyone having to attend other churches either where they felt led to go or where they felt welcome. One of the overseers and leaders came to give us a word of encouragement from the Lord and he reminded us of these two verses. Romans 29:11 and Jeremiah 11:29. He said to remember them like this: Romans 29:11 For the free gifts and His calling are irrevocable and then Jeremiah 11:29 I know the plans I have for you says Adonai, plan for well-being, not for bad things, so that you can have a hope and a future. We were seeds being sent forth to other churches as He distributed.

We also had a visit from a lovely friend before he left to go back to his home country of Australia, it was a lovely surprise to see him, as we had not had contact for a while. This was such a blessing as we seen him before we went to Rome for a holiday.

We are always in awe of how God blesses us, and we were able to go to Rome for a lovely break and also to see ST. Paul's Basilica along with Stephen's Basilica. One of my favourite things is to put faces to names and I was able to do that in Rome. We also managed to see a statue of St. Peter.

I had a wonderful birthday present seeing Rome and being with my wonderful husband. The Lord blessed us out of our socks.

Today is the day of Pentecost on the church calendar and my birthday> I do not know if there is any significance in all of this, but I do know that the number nine is the time of gestation prophetically.

It is the first day back at work and I felt the Lord was asking me to step down from leading worship and that I would be speaking my testimony to women's groups, telling them of His goodness and what He has done in our lives as an encouragement to them. So now to wait for the next step.

1 Corinthians 13:4-5 Love suffers long and is kind, love does not envy, love does not parade itself, is not puffed up, does not behave rudely, does not seek its own, is not provoked, thinks no evil.

As I spoke to our worship coordinator, asking him to release me from the worship group, I had such a beautiful touch from the Lord and so much peace came upon me. I am a worshipper and love to worship my Lord but as I said to God, "You put me on the platform and You can take me off." I believe that when God closes a door, then He will open a new door.

Psalm 68:5 Sing to God, sing praises to His Name, extol Him who rides on the clouds by

His Name—YAH and be glad in His presence.

Isaiah 40:31 ...but those who hope in Adonai will renew their strength, they will soar aloft as with eagles' wings, when they are running they won't grow weary, when they are walking they won't get tired.

As God has always referred to my heart as a garden, I have just gone through a difficult season and He is reminding me that the ground needs to be prepared for the planting of new seed. I used to wonder about these seasons but now realise that He is doing a new thing in my heart and preparing it for the new thing. It does not make those seasons any better, but I think that once we realise what God is doing it helps us to press on and press into Him.

This morning, a friend that I have not seen for such a long time said that she had a word for me. The word was, It is time to give birth. I knew what she meant straight away and I believed it was a confirmation of what God had already laid on my heart. It aligned perfectly with words that a friend in Canada had also given me about Wales.

Exodus 14:14 Adonai will do battle for you, just calm yourselves down.

1 Peter 3:12 For Adonai keeps His eyes on the righteous and His ears are open to their prayers, but the Face of Adonai is against those who do evil things.

Today the Lord gave me revelation of standing. I stand under God and when I humble myself under His mighty hand, my stance is to stand. I stand under His authority and when He gives me a word to speak, I find myself standing under His anointing and presence.

As I was reading my devotional today, it posed the question, Why does God cause His Spirit's voice to be difficult to hear on times?

I believe this is part of the answer as I was drawn to this reading. My Pastor has a saying that if it was easy then everybody would do it. Even some of Jesus' disciples left because they thought it was too hard.

John 1:5 They will never (on any account) follow a stranger but will run away from him because they do not know the voice of a stranger or recognise their call.

This quote by Lois T from Sitting at the Feet of Rabbi Jesus.

'Anything attained after enduring high levels of difficulty will always be highly respected, greatly admired and deeply cherished. Difficulty is a blessing. We learn to recognise the Holy Spirit – relationship – no short cut – no secret.'[22]

When you know the Holy Spirit, you won't follow a stranger.

Romans 8:26. Similarly, the Spirit helps us in our weakness for we don't know how to pray the way we should, but the Spirit, Himself, pleads on our behalf with groanings too deep for words.

---

[22] Spangler, Ann & Tverberg, Lois: Sitting at the Feet of Rabbi Jesus, Zondervan, 2009

Hebrews 12:11. Now all discipline while it is happening does indeed seem painful, not enjoyable but for those who have been trained by it, it later produces it is peaceful fruit that is righteousness.

Having had a neck and back operation quite a while ago, I still find it hard to slow down when I know there is work to be done. Then I suffer physically when I have overstepped my boundaries, I believe God is trying to slow me down a bit. I have a wonderful team of young people to work with me so after a very busy few months I am feeling the strain and the pain.

This morning my team prayed for me, and the pain left, discipline does indeed seem painful, but I am grateful to God that He shows us these things.

I am now being obedient and not overstepping my boundaries, especially when I think like a thirty-year-old but have the body of an over sixty's model.

I thank the Lord for His word that He reminds of on occasion in Proverbs, His word is strength to my bones, health to my flesh and grace to my neck.

The word I received from the Lord through a friend was this.

As a fresh bunch of flowers need refreshing daily, we also need refreshing daily through His word.

How true is that. Jesus went to the Father daily to pray so how much more do we need to do the same; spending time with Him to keep us fresh daily.

CHAPTER THIRTY-TWO | **In the Waiting Room**

As I was reflecting this morning, I realised that I am in the waiting room.

I do not know about you, but I really find it hard to wait. I know what has to happen but then I sit in the waiting room and think about what could or might happen, then I come to my senses and stop myself thinking the worse.

We probably all get there at one point or another but we need to learn to take those thoughts captive unto the obedience of Christ. It is an ongoing process, as the enemy never gives up.

Sermons often speak to us as we listen, and this morning was one of those mornings. I was watching a teaching by Pastor Joel Osteen entitled, It is Worth the Wait.[23]

Pastor Joel was saying that while we are in the waiting room, God is doing something in us and preparing us. He likened it to the weight room in a gym.

Patience, he says, is developed in the weight room. Just as our muscles do not develop over-night, so our patience does not develop overnight, it takes time.

---

[23] https://sermons.love/joel-osteen/4632-joel-osteen-its-worth-the-wait.html

We need to be in the wait-room with a good attitude, do not discount the wait- room, and to be the best we can be where we are because God is preparing us for what He has in mind for us.

We are interested in the destination, but God is interested in the journey.

it is not an easy place to be but it is worth it, and as I was listening and watching Joel Osteen's teaching, it was as if Jesus was speaking to me.

James 1:4 Let patience have it is perfect work that you may be perfect and complete, lacking nothing.

I am sure that many of us feel like that when we think nothing is happening.

We will be speaking to somebody, and God quickens our heart as if He is standing in front of us saying, "Wait child, I have not forgotten you."

Please be encouraged that God has not forgotten you either, be the best you that you can be for Him, where you are and, in His time, He will reward you.

A word of encouragement from a dear friend.

My treasure, look to Me and live; know that I have this situation in hand. I am accomplishing My purposes in and through it. Relax, I am causing you to do what I desire of you, the only thing you need to change is your consternation-(a feeling of anxiety or dismay, typically at something unexpected.)

Relax and be still and know that I am God.

You do not have this situation in hand because that is My job, know that I am God, I am causing things to unfold as is best, know also that I will keep you safe, so relax, be happy and go to sleep.'

I thanked the Lord for this word as I had gone through a few restless nights that I could not sleep and His heart is always to encourage us and give us peace.

Proverbs 19:21 One can devise many plans in one's mind, but Adonai's plan will prevail.

God also gave me a picture of my heart; it was gold — refined like gold. I was walking on a golden road.

Colossians 13:23-24 Whatever you do, put yourself into it as those who are not merely serving other people but the Lord. Remember that as your reward you will receive the inheritance from the Lord, you are slaving for the Lord, for the Messiah.

The song, Here's my heart Lord, speak what is true,[24] came to mind. I answered, "Here's my heart Lord." I was not surprised as He often speaks to me through songs, it took me a while to recognise this, but I learned to take note of the words of the songs that would come from deep down in my heart.

I believe the Lord said, "Are you ready? Are you ready for the blessings?"

So, I pose the question, How does God speak to you? I wonder how many of you reading this would say that God does not speak to you. I think sometimes the problem is that we do not recognise when God is

---

[24] Jason Ingram*/Louie Giglio/Chris Tomlin, Here is My Heart, Essential Music, 2013, UK

speaking to us. He does not speak to everyone the same, but He does speak.

I saw a stone drop into a very still pond and the water rippled out from that point. I believe that He was showing me the ripple effect of the blessings that God is sending for everyone at Pierrepont and that I should share it with the leaders.

Habakkuk 2:2 God said to write down the vision, write it clearly so that even a runner can read it, for it is meant for an appointed time, it speaks of the end and does not lie.

We thank the Lord for the increase, and we give You the whole of the First Fruits, we praise You Lord God, Lord Jesus and Holy Spirit.

Proverbs 3:9 (The Message) Honour God with everything you own, give Him the First and the best, your barns will burst your wine vats will brim over.

I believe that when we honour God with our substance, He will honour us.

As I walk through this year, I am in awe of how much the Lord teaches us and even if we forget things, the Holy Spirit reminds us.

Sometimes the words that He gives me to speak are so strong in my heart that there could be no denying that the Lord wants to use my mouth. it is a privilege but I always make sure that the word is to be given for everyone and not just for me; again, this is something I have learned to do over the years, and it takes time and training. I have also learned that when God gives a revelation the enemy is not far behind trying to discount what God has said.

This morning I woke up at precisely 3:33am and as I sat with Him, this verse came to mind.

Nehemiah 3:33. But when Sanballat heard that they were rebuilding the wall, he was furious, greatly enraged, he ridiculed the Judeans.

When we are going for God and He has taken us up to a new level, the enemy will always try to discourage us. That is when we need to stand our ground and keep standing. Keep standing on what God had shown or said.

Many years ago, when I was newly born again, I made a vow to God that I would give up chocolate after He had shown me it was an idol in my life. I had only been born again for a short while, so I immediately thought I had to give up eating chocolate. I was very happy to do so, and the one thing that I asked the Lord was to help me by taking away the desire for chocolate, which He did. From that time onwards, I did not eat chocolate or anything containing chocolate. That was around nine or ten years ago, and until this year, I have kept my vow, with the Lord's help.

Today as I sat with Him, He suddenly brought to mind 1 Samuel 5:22. Does the Lord delight in burnt offerings as sacrifices as much as in obeying the voice of the Lord? To obey is better than the fat of rams.

It was then that I heard that still small voice saying that He was releasing me from my vow. I asked Him for confirmation and a while later I received it through somebody that I was mentoring. It took me a while to have chocolate, but I remember it was Easter and the first chocolate I ate was a Cadbury's Creme Egg® and I must say it was delicious.

I had not eaten it for such a long time and it did not bother me as I really meant the vow that I had made, but God was gracious and almost ten year later, He released me from the vow. I cannot tell you why, but I knew that He had. I believe it was because it was no longer an idol!

The scripture God gave me was Hosea 6:6 For I desire steadfast love and not sacrifice, the knowledge of God rather than burnt offerings.

I thanked Him and suddenly the sunshine flooded into the room brightly and I knew in my heart that He was saying to me, I am here. I have waited for a long time, and He has shown me His heart and chocolate is no longer an idol.

2 Corinthians 3:17 Now Adonai in this text means the Spirit and where the Spirit of Adonai is, there is freedom, and I had been set free.

Later on, we went to Wales again to visit a Pastor friend to catch up with them, they are originally from China and now Pastor in Swansea, and we keep in touch and pray for each other often.

We had a good rest and today we had the privilege of praying for a homeless guy in town, we did not catch many fish, but our nets are still in the water.

We have been waiting patiently for God to direct us to Wales but all the doors up to now seem to be closed. Oh well! Maybe next year will be the right time.

Still, we thank God for all that He has done this year and maybe next year will be even better.

This morning as I listened to my devotional, this really touched my heart...

... Whenever you feel poor and powerless, the resurrected Christ is looking to reveal His power through you. All the areas of your life that feel insignificant are exactly where Christ is looking to do another resurrection miracle.

Isaiah 40:29 He gives power to the weak and to those who have no might, He increases strength.

2 Corinthians 2:9 My grace is enough for you, for My power is brought to perfection in weakness, therefore I am very happy to boast about my weakness in order that the Messiah's power will rest upon me.

Give thanks to Adonai for He is good for His grace continues forever.

As we have gone through this year, things have come against us, trials etc. BUT

GOD… is always faithful to get us through to the other side.

One of my favourite verses; that He gave me to use as a sword is Psalm 27:13 I would have lost heart had I not believed that I would see the goodness of God in the land of the living.

I use my sword often… Amen.

So, at the end of another year, I am reminded that God has not forgotten us, and He never will, He has promised that He will be with us always even to the end of the age.

My prayer is that whoever reads this book will be encouraged and know who you are in Him and who He is in you, for greater is He that is in us than he who is in the world.

I bless you with all God's blessings and all His Spiritual blessings that He wants to pour out on your life.

He is an amazing Father, a Mighty God and there is no one like Him. I pray that you will know Him more and more.

A number of years back, God gave me a word that He would build us a house and so as we wait on Him, I hope to share the next adventure when it is the right time, and when we get to Wales.

Blessings upon blessings,

Susannah

May the Lord bless you and keep you, May His face shine upon you, May His countenance be upon you, and may He give you peace.

Numbers 6:24-26

www.ingramcontent.com/pod-product-compliance
Lightning Source LLC
Chambersburg PA
CBHW041316110526
44591CB00021B/2807